PRAISE FOR *HE IS ENOUGH*

Looking for a way to study the Bible no matter your season of life? Look no further than Asheritah's *He Is Enough*. As a busy mom of four kids, I especially appreciated how this study is formatted to give me both "snacks" to meditate on all during my day and "feasts" on God's Word when time allows.

ERIN ODOM

Author of *More Than Just Making It* and *You Can Stay Home with Your Kids*
Creator of The Humbled Homemaker blog

I'm so grateful there are women like Asheritah in my generation—who know the Word, who crave the Word, who teach the Word well. I fully endorse this study—terrific both for individual or a small group study!

JESSICA SMARTT

Author/creator of "Smartter" Each Day

Working through *He Is Enough* felt like sitting down with Asheritah at a kitchen table over coffee, with Bibles open and kids playing in the background. The tone is relatable, warm, and real, and the content is deeply nourishing and challenging. This Bible study has been the ushering into the presence of God that I was longing for during a stressful season of life. I didn't know I had so much to learn from what was already one of my favorite books, Colossians!

KATIE BENNETT

Author of *Heavenly Minded Mom* and creator of Embracing a Simpler Life

Finally a Bible study made for women in different seasons of life! The lessons found in the book of Colossians and in *He Is Enough* are rich. They will challenge you to connect the struggles of your daily grind to God's sufficiency, and they will lead you to correct your wrong thinking with scriptural truths that are rooted in the grace and power of Jesus. If you're ready to understand and embrace the life-altering fullness offered to you in Christ, then don't hesitate to take this sacred walk with Asheritah.

GWEN SMITH

Cofounder of *Girlfriends in God*, speaker, worship leader, and author of *I Want It All* and *Broken into Beautiful*

HE IS ENOUGH

LIVING IN THE *fullness* OF JESUS

A 6-Week Bible Study on Colossians

ASHERITAH CIUCIU

MOODY PUBLISHERS

CHICAGO

© 2018 by

ASHERITAH CIUCIU

Published in association with Literary Agent Tawny Johnson of D.C. Jacobson and Associates, PO Box 80945, Portland, OR 97280. www.dcjacobson.com.

Edited by Pamela J. Pugh
Interior design: Erik M. Peterson
Cover design: Dean Renninger
Cover illustration of watercolor grapes copyright © 2018 by Kuzmina Aleksandra / Shutterstock (336964424). All rights reserved.
Verse lettering by Sue Fehlberg and Kelsey Fehlberg.
Author photo: Ashley McComb

ISBN: 978-0-8024-1686-5

We hope you enjoy this book from Moody Publishers. Our goal is to provide high-quality, thought-provoking books and products that connect truth to your real needs and challenges. For more information on other books and products written and produced from a biblical perspective, write to:

Moody Publishers
820 N. LaSalle Boulevard
Chicago, IL 60610

1 3 5 7 9 10 8 6 4 2

Printed in the United States of America

To Carmen, my friend, mentor, and ministry partner.
Thank you for always pointing me to Jesus. He is enough.

CONTENTS

WHY STUDY COLOSSIANS?

"For in Christ all the fullness of the Deity lives in bodily form, and in Christ you have been brought to fullness." COLOSSIANS 2:9-10a

You can't get away from it.

From the moment we blearily scroll through our newsfeed in the morning to the moment we rest our heads on the pillow at night, we're bombarded with sales pitches promising a fuller life. Whether it's thicker hair, washboard abs, smoother skin, burgeoning finances, obedient kids, or hip accessories, the world offers us plenty of opportunities to experience the full life.

But the answer lies not in six low payments of only $19.99 a month . . . but in a personal relationship with Jesus. And by that I don't mean saying a prayer in a church basement years ago, although that may have been a great beginning. I mean an active, growing, fruitful life united with Jesus, filled with the Spirit, and resting in the Father.

Because here's the problem: We might say we believe that Christ is enough, but do we really live that out? Do we understand the theological richness of our union with Jesus? *Do we live as those who are truly full, having everything we need already fulfilled in Christ?* Or do we keep chasing the latest diet, the newest purse, or the hottest multilevel marketing opportunity?

Please hear me: there's nothing inherently wrong with those things, but we need to understand that they'll never really satisfy. As long as we keep reaching for earthly fulfillment, we'll continue to feel empty, longing for more. But when we discover the fullness of the riches that are ours in Christ Jesus—when we realize that our greatest gift is Jesus Christ Himself—we will begin living out the reality of that fullness that is already ours in Him.

Everything we need we already have in Jesus.

The first-century church of Colossae faced these same issues. Sure, theirs might not have been packaged as sleek sales pitches on high-resolution screens, but the root issue was the same: is Jesus really enough, or do we need something else, something more in order to experience the full life?

There were smooth talkers even then, promising secret knowledge that would lead to spiritual transcendence available to the elite few. And there were others who imposed heavy rules and regulations, promising spiritual refinement to those who checked all the right boxes.

It was tempting to try it out. What could it hurt? But in this short letter, Paul packs a punch. No, you don't need secret knowledge. No, you don't need more rules. No, you don't need more stuff. You need Jesus. And if you have Jesus, you have all you need.

Jesus is enough for your salvation. He is enough for your family. He is enough for your finances. He is enough for your health. He is enough for your career. He is enough for your fears, your hopes, your burdens, and your future.

He is enough.

Are you ready to shed cheap imitations and begin living out the fullness that is yours in Christ Jesus?

MAKING THE MOST OF THIS STUDY

I'm so glad you picked up this Bible study, because over the next few weeks we're going to uncover the riches of Christ Jesus and discover how to live in His fullness. If you stick with me through our study of Colossians, your life *will* be transformed. Because God's Word never returns to Him void. But let's be honest: "I'm doing a Bible study" can be easier said than done.

It's like trying to eat healthy. Most of us know what we should eat and how often, but finding the time to prepare nutritious meals and actually sitting down to eat them can be a challenge. It's tempting to think that if we can't eat healthfully, we might as well skip the meal altogether (or grab a candy bar). Am I right?

We all know this: it's better to grab a nutritious snack than skip a meal. Ask any nutritionist: there's great value in eating small but regular meals throughout the day. (I'm talking healthy snacks here, not candy bars, much to our collective chagrin.)

The same is true when it comes to feeding our souls. Many of us may be tempted to skip Bible study altogether if we can't fit in a 30- to 45-minute inductive study of Scripture. But we're better off grabbing a bite of Scripture or a moment of prayer than completely ignoring our spiritual nutrition.

Listen to an explanation of the Snack and FEAST ways to read the Bible in a short interview on Moody Radio. Go to **myOneThingAlone.com/snack-interview**.

After all, there's no command in the Bible that states, "Thou shalt start each morning with an hour of inductive Bible study and prayer." In fact, quite the opposite is true: throughout biblical times, we find great variety and creativity in the ways God's people approached Him from morning through night—praying honest prayers saturated with Scripture, reciting memorized Scripture, offering worshipful songs filled with Scripture, and yes, even reading Scripture. And that's okay.

Because while we may consume Scripture in different ways in different seasons, nothing can replace God's Word in our lives. It is our daily bread, our spiritual sustenance

> Then Jesus declared, "I am the bread of life. Whoever comes to me will never go hungry, and whoever believes in me will never be thirsty."
> JOHN 6:35

As we nourish our souls in God's presence, His Bread of Life will both satisfy us and make us hunger for more. But whether we eat this spiritual fare in one big meal or in small bites throughout the day is entirely up to us, and this may look different from month to month or even from day to day.

So I've structured this Bible study to invite you—whatever season of life you're in—to feed your soul with the daily bread of God's Word.

Each week we'll begin with a short introduction setting up the week's theme, followed by a memory verse coloring page. Throughout this book you'll find many prompts to creatively engage the Word and worship Jesus, and those coloring pages are a way to do just that; as you color, meditate on the words and commit them to memory. What follows are five days of Bible study prompts in Snack and FEAST sections, and at the very end, a weekend reflection to help you summarize and internalize what you've learned.

If three minutes is all you have, grab the daily *Snack on the Go*. It's a morsel of Scripture that you can consume quickly and reflect on all day long. It will give you energy boosts to keep you going rather than starving yourself spiritually.

If you have more time, sit down to *FEAST at the Table* on Scripture. Each day I'll walk you through an inductive study of the daily passage, complete with observation, interpretation, application, and adoration. By *FEASTing* on God's Word each day, you'll become more confident in your ability to study the Bible for yourself, and by the end of this study, you'll be ready to apply the *FEAST* method to any passage of Scripture.

I developed and tested the FEAST Bible study method a few years ago with the myOneThingAlone.com community, an online sisterhood that loves Jesus and grows deeper with Him through creative spiritual disciplines. Our very first study was on the book of Colossians (which led to this book you hold in your hands), and we discovered that whether we were *snacking* or *FEASTing*, the daily discipline of opening God's Word led to deeper joy in His presence. God was faithful to His promise, taking our *snacks* and *FEASTs* and multiplying them to feed our souls. I hope you'll find the same to be true in your life as well.

We will delve more deeply into the FEAST method in the first week, but just to give you a quick overview, each letter represents a step in inductive Bible study:

F: Focus on God (open in prayer)

E: Engage the text (read and observe Scripture)

A: Assess the main idea (interpret the meaning)

S: Spark transformation (apply the main idea to your life)

T: Turn to God in worship (respond with adoration)

Don't worry; it's easier than it looks right now, and I'll walk you through it every step of the way. In fact, I've provided a Daily Main Ideas Guide on page 227 in case you get stuck. And for the record, you don't have to fill in every blank or answer every question—if you sense the Holy Spirit leading in another direction, follow His lead! You may find Him prodding you to look up other verses than those that are suggested in this guide. You might want to pause in the middle of your study for a time of spontaneous worship. Or you might find Him convicting you of a phone call you need to make or a person you need to pray for right then and there. Follow where He leads. He knows what you need better than anyone else.

If you find that one day you don't have time to *FEAST*—it's okay. Just grab the *snack* for that day, and return to *FEASTing* when you have the time.

If you're leading this study, you'll find a devotional guide called "Serving and Leading" written specifically for women in ministry to supplement your own personal study of the text. And don't feel like you need an official title to qualify for this role. If you're leading in any capacity, even if it's a group of friends around your kitchen table, you'll find this section especially helpful.

Above all, my prayer is that through this study you'll be filled up with knowledge and love of Jesus, growing to understand all the ways that His supremacy, sufficiency, and beauty overflow into the mundane tasks of your life, so that you may please Him in everything you do, fully aware of His powerful strength, patience, and joy at work in you even right this very moment. Because we desperately need Jesus. And He is enough.

With much joy,

Asheritah

SOME BACKGROUND ON COLOSSIANS

Sadly, many Christian congregations are often shaped more by the latest ideas or hot topics circulating *about* the faith than the timeless truth of God's revealed word in the Bible. But this isn't a new problem—it's as old as the church itself, as we'll see in Colossians. Over the next few weeks, we'll discover that Paul wrote this letter to respond to false teachings that were creeping into the church in Colossae. We'll see how he points not just to God's Word in general, but to God's Word made flesh in Jesus Christ; Christ alone is enough for all who believe in Him.

But before we begin studying the text closely, let's dig a little bit into the history of this church to better understand who Paul was addressing and what prompted him to write his letter to this church in Colossae in the first place.

The city of Colossae was located in the southwest region of what is now modern-day Turkey, right on one of the great trade routes of the ancient world. Once a thriving center of commerce, Colossae had been quite cosmopolitan in its day, but by the time Paul wrote his letter around AD 60, the city had been declining in importance and prominence. However, some of Colossae's residual influence was still felt in the eclectic mix of cultures found in the area, including Greek, Roman, and Jewish religions. This unique blend of pagan and Jewish influences affected the spiritual health of the Christians living in Colossae, as we'll see Paul address both directly and indirectly.

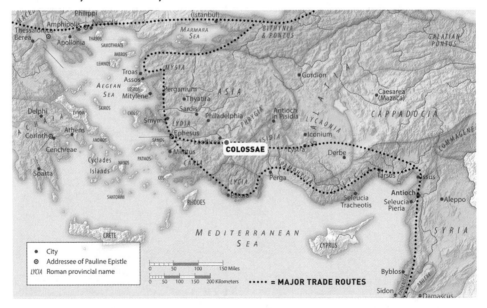

Based on our knowledge of Paul's missionary journeys, it's unlikely that Paul ever visited Colossae in person. However, there's good reason to believe that he led Epaphras to faith through his three-year preaching ministry in Ephesus[1] (Acts 19:10), and that Epaphras later returned to his hometown in Colossae to preach the good news to his fellow neighbors (Col. 1:7, 4:12). This would explain why Paul's letter to the Colossians is filled with pastoral concern and warmth, based on his closeness to Epaphras and his eagerness to address the issues the congregation was facing even though he had never met them in person.

While most of Paul's letters were written in direct response to particular issues the receiving church was facing, it's a bit more difficult to identify what those issues were in the Colossian church. The two major clues we can use to decipher the needs of the Colossian church are:

1. The unhealthy practices Paul brings up: the Jewish observance of food and drink laws, holy days, and circumcision, and the pagan practices of angel worship, secret knowledge, and exaltation of human wisdom and traditions.

2. The doctrines Paul emphasizes throughout his short letter: the centrality, fullness, and sufficiency of the person and work of Jesus Christ.

As you begin studying the book of Colossians, remember that even though the Bible is written *for* us, it wasn't written *to* us. This letter was written at a particular time in history for a particular group of people dealing with particular problems.

So we'll be careful to observe the text in its proper context and to interpret the meaning for the original audience first. Then, only after careful interpretation, will we bring the main truth to apply to our own lives as twenty-first-century women. Because the whole point of Bible information is to lead to God-adoration and spiritual transformation, that we might fulfill Jesus' greatest commandments: to love God and to love others (Matt. 22:37–40).

Are you ready?

Here we go.

praying through Christ

The gospel is bearing fruit and growing throughout the whole world.
COLOSSIANS 1:6b

How do you come to know God? How do you access His will and wisdom?

Whether you realize it or not, how you answer those questions reveals as much about your relationship with Jesus as it does about your theology. And this isn't a new discussion . . . it's been brewing for thousands of years, as shown in Paul's opening prayer in his letter to the Colossians.

Paul begins his letter with two prayers, each of which reveals his confidence in Christ alone for the work of the gospel in the church in Colossae. As we'll study this week, these prayers lay the groundwork for the rest of the letter, as every other concern Paul brings up comes back to his confidence expressed in these two prayers.

At the heart of these prayers—and indeed this entire letter—is Paul's earnest desire that the Colossians come to rest in the sufficiency of Jesus Christ's finished work on the cross and the continued work of His Spirit in and through the lives of those who believe in Him. He is enough, both for saving us and securing us for eternity.

Spoiler alert: it's not our good works and it's not some secret knowledge that lead us to God, as the heretics in Colossae were teaching. It's Jesus Christ Himself. He

is enough. It's in Christ alone that we come to know God, and it's through Him alone that we are transformed and made fruitful for God's glory. It's only in getting to know Jesus more that we will experience the fullness of God's presence as we yearn for it.

As you begin this study, pause to examine your heart: Do you desire Jesus more than anything? Are you hungry to know Him more through His Word?

Be honest with yourself and with God. He already knows your heart. If the answer is, "Umm, not really," then tell Him so. And then ask Him to stir in you a hunger for Him.

If the answer is yes, then thank Him for placing that desire in you (because we know it only comes from Him), and ask Him to grow that hunger and thirst for Him. Because Jesus promises, "Blessed are those who hunger and thirst for righteousness, for they will be filled" (Matt. 5:6).

Either way, friend, we are in for the adventure of a lifetime.

Let's dig in.

IN THE SAME WAY, the gospel is bearing fruit and Growing throughout the Whole World.

COLOSSIANS 1:6b

WEEK 1 | DAY 1

SNACK ON THE GO

As a missionary to the Gentiles, Paul was frequently traveling and starting churches throughout Asia minor, as well as discipling others, like Epaphras, to go and start other churches throughout the region (1:7).

The gospel thus spread throughout the Roman empire, as followers of Jesus shared the good news with those they encountered, and when several people believed, they came together to form a church. Many of these first-century churches were small groups of people, tiny compared to most contemporary churches today, and lacking the liturgy and structure to their services that are familiar to us. Several of the apostles wrote letters to encourage these believers to continue in the way of Christ and to refute false teachings that were infiltrating the churches; these letters were read out loud first in the recipient church and then circulated among the surrounding churches (see Col. 4:16).

Today, we have the luxury of owning personal copies of these letters, holding them in our hands, lining our bookshelves with these pages. But often we lack the zeal of those first-century believers to read and share the truths found within these epistles.

Write out your own prayer for this study, asking God to awaken within you a hunger and thirst for His Word and His presence in your life.

Use Jeremiah 15:16 (NLT) as a starting point: "When I discovered your words, I devoured them. They are my joy and my heart's delight, for I bear your name, O Lord God of Heaven's Armies."

> Father God, Awaken a hunger in me. Stir me to ever thirst for more of your words. Cause me to crave time with you and study about you

FEAST AT THE TABLE

FOCUS ON GOD

Open your Bible to Psalm 119:10. Write it out as a prayer to the Lord as you begin your study of His Word today.

> With my whole heart I seek you let me not wander from your commandments

Are you a visual learner? Go to **myOneThingAlone.com/quickstart** to watch a short video tutorial on the FEAST Bible study method within our Bible Study Quickstart Guide.

ENGAGE THE TEXT

Handwritten at top right: Romans, Corinthians, Galatians, Philippians, Thessalonians, Philemon, Ephesians, Colossians, Timothy, Titus

Read Colossians. Yep, the whole book. Out loud. (It only takes about fifteen minutes. I timed myself.) As you read, imagine yourself seated among those first-century believers.

What themes are repeated over and over again? What stands out to you as you read?

Handwritten:
① Thanksgiving + prayer / Supremacy of Christ
② Alive in Christ / Let no one disqualify you
③ Living as those made alive in Christ / Instructions for Christian Households
④ Further Instructions / final greetings

Who wrote this letter (see 1:1 and 4:18)? What do you already know about the author?

Handwritten:
Paul / Tribe of Benjamin / Roman citizen / born Saul - Roman citizen, Jew, persecuted Christians, Jesus appeared, Ananias restored his sight, Preached in Syria, Asia Minor, Europe, sent to Rome / executed

Who was it written to (see 1:2)?

Handwritten: To the saints + faithful brothers in Christ at Colossae

What do we know about this church (see 1:3–8)?

Handwritten: Faith, love, lead + founded by Epaphras, love in the Spirit

According to 1:7–8, who planted this church?

Handwritten: Epaphras our beloved fellow servant

ASSESS THE MAIN IDEA

Reread the historical background (in the introduction of this study) to familiarize yourself with the Colossians' culture, and write down three to five observations about the historical setting. *Greek, Roman, Jewish cultures / trading economy*

Based on what you've learned about the historical background, write down a few ways the original audience is similar to you, and a few ways they are different. *melting pot over several religions*

Write out the main idea of Colossians, as you understand it today, in a single sentence. *Christ is center of universe not only active creator but also recept of creation — be man, flesh*

SPARK TRANSFORMATION

Jesus is sovereign head of church reconciled all with his death

One of the main themes of Colossians is that Jesus Christ is supreme and sufficient. In the coming weeks, we'll look at what that means in our lives in specific ways, but for now, spend a few minutes asking the Holy Spirit to reveal areas in your life in which you haven't believed that Christ is enough. If He shows you anything specific, feel free to write it down; but even if not, make this your daily prayer:

Lord Jesus, You are enough for me, and You are all I need. Please show me how to live out this truth in the coming weeks.

TURN TO GOD IN WORSHIP

As you read Colossians today, you may have noticed that it includes several beautiful passages that point to Christ's sufficiency. Use one of them as a guide to worship, personalizing the passage and praising Jesus for the ways He is enough for those who believe.

In the space below, list out the letters of the alphabet, from A to Z, and write down His attributes, at least one for each letter. Then take some time to worship God for all He is, using the book of Colossians for inspiration.

For example, you might begin like this:

Dear God, I praise You because You are *almighty* and *attentive* to every detail in the universe. Jesus, You are the *Author* and *Finisher* of my faith and *awesome* in power.

You are *bountiful* in Your gifts and *brilliant* in splendor and glory.

You are the *Creator* of all things, the *Christ* who saves us from our sins, and the *Coming One* who will take us home to be with You.

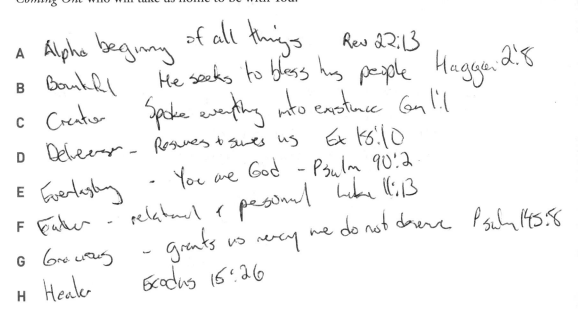

A Alpha beginning of all things   Rev 22:13

B Bountiful   He seeks to bless his people   Haggai 2:8

C Creator   Spoke everything into existence   Gen 1:1

D Deliverer - Rescues & saves us   Ex 15:10

E Everlasting   - You are God - Psalm 90:2

F Father - relational & personal   Luke 11:13

G Gracious   - grants us mercy we do not deserve   Psalm 145:8

H Healer   Exodus 15:26

I Infinite Psalm 147:5
J Just Isa 45:21
K King Rev 19:4
L Lion & Lamb Rev 5:5
M Merciful Messiah Micah 7:18-19
N Nurturing Psalm 82:2-3
O Omnipotent Rev 19:6
P Pure & holy Psalm 24:3-4
Q Quiet 1 Kings 19:12
R Righteous Job 4:17
S Savior Matt 1:21
T True Rev 22:6
U Unchanging Heb 7:24
V Victorious 1 Chr 29:11
W Wise Psalm 136:5
X Xerophilous - flourishes in even the driest of places living water John 4:13-14
Y Yahweh Ex 3:14 I am who I am
Z Zealous - desires us to know Him Joel 2:18

Praise Him for all of His wonderful ways, and use this list as a worship prompt throughout the week, turning your thoughts to worship whenever you see the alphabet.

WEEK 1 | DAY 2

SNACK ON THE GO

We live in a hectic world. There's hardly a moment of silence from the moment we wake up to the moment we close our eyes to sleep. And yet, it's in the midst of this busyness that our heavenly Father wants to speak to us, to remind us of who He is and who we are in Him.

Open your Bible to Colossians 1:1–2, and read these verses out loud. Write down the following:

How Paul describes God:

How Paul describes himself:

How he describes the believers in Colossae:

What one word or phrase jumps out to you? Write it in the space below. Why do you think that is connecting with your heart today?

Ask the Lord to help you believe that what He says is true. Then consider writing that word or phrase on your wrist, so you can see it and be reminded of your Scripture Snack throughout the day. Ask the Holy Spirit to continue to teach you what His Word means, and meditate on His truth, allowing it to shape your life.

FEAST AT THE TABLE

FOCUS ON GOD

Open your Bible to Psalm 119:11. Write it out as a prayer to the Lord as you begin your study of His Word today.

ENGAGE THE TEXT

Read Colossians 1:1–2 out loud, and then write it in the space below.

Write down anything that immediately stands out to you.

How does Paul describe himself in verse 1? What does this say about his identity in Christ?

We begin our study of Colossians with a startling description of the church members. How does Paul describe the Colossians?

What do each of those terms mean? (If you're unsure, you can use a regular dictionary or find a Bible dictionary online.) Define them in the space below.

Find Bible dictionaries and commentaries at **biblestudytools.com** or **biblegateway.com**.

What is Paul doing by calling them "brothers and sisters in Christ"?

What type of familial bond holds them together?

What salutation does Paul open with?

What do each of those words mean?

How does Paul refer to God in this passage? What is the significance of that term?

What do you learn about God in this text?

ASSESS THE MAIN IDEA

What did this mean to the original audience?

Write out the main idea of this passage in a single sentence. Make it precise, concise, and memorable.

SPARK TRANSFORMATION

When you think of yourself, what words immediately come to mind?

Would you consider yourself holy? Faithful? Why or why not?

As you begin this study of Colossians, write a prayer below asking God to search your heart and help you identify any false labels you may be wearing. Ask Him to remove those lies and to write on your heart your new identity in Christ Jesus.

TURN TO GOD IN WORSHIP

Paul begins his letter by blessing the Colossians with the grace and peace that come from God, whom he calls "our Father." As you wrap up your time in the study of Scripture, turn your heart to praise God, who has called you to be His child, and who makes you holy and faithful in Christ, a member of His family. Thank Him for being the giver of all grace, and the One who speaks peace over the most tumultuous storms of life. End by being still before Him, receiving His fatherly love toward you.

If you'd like, you can want write down your prayer in the space below.

WEEK 1 | DAY 3

SNACK ON THE GO

Paul begins most of his letters, including this one to the Colossians, with thanks to God for His work in the lives of believers. Although Paul speaks highly of the faith, hope, and love displayed by the church in Colossae, he never attributes these characteristics to human effort but rather always points to God, who is the source of these virtues:

> We always thank God, the Father of our Lord Jesus Christ, when we pray for you, because we have heard of your faith in Christ Jesus and of the love you have for all God's people. COLOSSIANS 1:3–4

Take a moment to reflect on your own life and recognize the ways God is working in you. What can you thank Him for today? Write a prayer of thanksgiving to Him below or in your journal.

FEAST AT THE TABLE

FOCUS ON GOD

Open your Bible to Psalm 119:14. Write it out as a prayer to the Lord as you begin your study of His Word today.

ENGAGE THE TEXT

Read Colossians 1:3–8 and write it below.

Write down whatever jumps out to you in the text.

What are Paul and Timothy thankful for?

What words are repeated in this text, and how does each new mention of the word add more nuance to its meaning?

What are the main markers of the believers in Colossae?

How are faith and love interwoven in this text?

How does hope (v. 5) relate to faith and love (see also Titus 1:2)?

According to verses 5 and 6, what does the gospel do wherever it goes?

The verb in the phrase "the gospel is bearing fruit and growing" in verse 6 is a present continuous passive tense verb in the Greek, which in plain English means the action is ongoing, with or without your participation. What does this verb choice communicate about the power of the gospel, apart from human intervention?

What effect has the gospel had in the church in Colossae?

This idea of bearing fruit, increasing, being fruitful, etc., is common in Scripture. Look up Mark 4:8 and Genesis 1:28. What connection points do you notice in these texts?

The phrase "your love in the Spirit" in verse 8 implies that the Holy Spirit is the source of Christian love. What other "fruit" (see v. 6) does the gospel empowered by the Holy Spirit bear in believers' lives (see Galatians 5:16–25)?

ASSESS THE MAIN IDEA

What is the gospel? In your own words, describe this good news Paul writes of, in one or two sentences.

Write out the main idea of this passage in a single sentence. Make it precise, concise, and memorable. (Consider the following question: What effect does the gospel have in the lives of believers?)

SPARK TRANSFORMATION

Have you believed the gospel of Jesus Christ? If not, or if you're not sure, take some time before going further in this study to read and understand the good news of Jesus Christ. If you're already a follower of Christ, review the truths of the gospel so you're comfortable sharing the good news with others.

Before I share the good news of the gospel of Jesus and show you the way to begin a relationship with Jesus, I have to start with the bad news.

The bad news is that we are all dead in our sins, having broken God's commandments and turned away from Him. And God is holy, set apart from anything sinful, so we cannot enter God's presence or have a relationship with Him in our sinful state. The payment for sin is death, eternal separation from God.

But the good news is that while we were still sinners, Christ died for us. God showed His love for us by sending His Son, Jesus Christ, to die for our sins. Though the wages of sin is death, the gift of God is eternal life in Christ Jesus our Lord. Salvation is a gift—we do not earn it or deserve it, but God gives it freely to all who believe in Him, and through Jesus we have peace with God.

But the good news gets even better! Jesus didn't remain dead—He came back to life on the third day, and God exalted Him to the highest place, and He rules as Lord over all. When we choose to accept Jesus' sacrifice on our behalf, we receive God's forgiveness of our sins, and we surrender control of our lives to Jesus.

Whether you're accepting Christ for the first time and committing your life to Him or you're already a believer, these verses are helpful to know and meditate on to more fully understand the great salvation message: **John 14:6; Romans 3:10–12; 5:1, 8; 6:23; 1 Corinthians 15:4; Ephesians 1:5; 2:4–5, 8–9; Philippians 2:9–11; Hebrews 4:16; 1 John 1:9; Jeremiah 29:13**.

What happens then is our dead spirits come to life, and we begin a relationship with God that continues for the rest of our lives and into eternity. We are adopted into God's family as His children, so we no longer fear God but instead run to Him as our Father. God welcomes us into His presence every day, and His Spirit lives inside us, empowering us to accomplish God's work here on earth and teaching us more and more about our heavenly Father. We can now boldly approach God's throne of grace to find help in our time of need. And though we may still miss the mark of God's perfection and holiness, when we confess our sins, God is faithful and just to forgive us our sins and purify us from all wrongdoing. He frees us to live the life that He created us to live, filled with amazing projects, dreams, and good works that God prepared in advance for us.

The Christian life is not a set of rules, but rather it's a relationship, and God wants us to grow deeper and deeper in our intimacy with Him by intentionally seeking Him every day. Though there is no three-step formula to Christian growth (after all, what relationship works that way?), there are spiritual disciplines that we can practice to open ourselves to God's work in us, as He grows us in spiritual maturity. The most common ones practiced by Christians throughout history include prayer, worship, reading the Bible, and gathering with other Christians in church.

If you want to begin a relationship with God, tell Him so in a simple prayer from your heart. Or, you can use the prayer below to guide you:

Dear God, I realize that I'm a sinner, and my sin separates me from You. I believe that Jesus Christ died for my sins, and that He rose again on the third day. I accept Jesus as the Savior and Lord of my life, and I believe, based on what You promised, that I am saved from my sins. Thank You for the gift of eternal life, for sending Your Spirit to live inside me, and for welcoming me into a relationship with You. Teach me how to grow deeper with You, and I look forward to an eternity of getting to know You more. Amen.

I encourage you to look up these Bible verses that I've included in the sidebar to cement these truths in your heart and mind.

How confident do you feel in your ability to articulate the gospel to others?

What effect does the gospel empowered by the Holy Spirit have on your life today? In what way(s) can you grow in faith, hope, and love?

TURN TO GOD IN WORSHIP

Without the Holy Spirit of God working in us, we are helpless. But when He works out in our lives the good news of Jesus' death and resurrection for our sins, He empowers us toward radical lives of continual transformation into the image of Jesus Christ. We cannot change on our own, but the Spirit of Jesus is more than sufficient to transform us. End your time of feasting by expressing your neediness to God. Open your life wide and declare to Him, "I need You!" Confess to Him the ways in which you have failed to show hope, faith, and love, and thank Him for His forgiveness and restoration (1 John 1:8–10). Then praise Jesus for being enough and caring enough to work out His hope, faith, and love in your life. Write a prayer of praise below.

WEEK 1 | DAY 4

SNACK ON THE GO

Oftentimes we'll tell friends, "I'll pray for you," with the best of intentions, but when it comes to actually praying for them, we're at a loss for words. What exactly should we pray? How do we lift our friends to God without reducing God to a genie-in-the-bottle who rushes to do our every whim? How can we learn to pray powerful, God-honoring prayers?

The answer comes in praying Scripture. Paul's letters are filled with powerful prayers, rich in theology and practical in applications, like this one in Colossians 1:9:

> We continually ask God to fill you with the knowledge of his will through all the wisdom and understanding that the Spirit gives.

When's the last time you prayed that for someone? Perhaps not in recent memory. And yet, we know and believe that God's Word is powerful, and it does not return to Him without producing the work it's intended to do, so let's begin praying Scripture over our lives.

Who is someone you can pray this passage for today? Rewrite the verse in your own words in the space below, inserting your friend's name as needed.

FEAST AT THE TABLE

FOCUS ON GOD

Open your Bible to Psalm 119:16. Write it out as a prayer to the Lord as you begin your study of His Word today.

ENGAGE THE TEXT

Read Colossians 1:9–12 out loud.

Write out the passage in the space below. If you enjoy grammar, try diagramming—it's enlightening, especially for Paul's long sentences. Look for nouns, verbs, adjectives, adverbs. But even if you don't like grammar, you can still map out this passage by main idea, secondary supporting ideas, clarifying ideas, and so on. Make this as simple or complex as you like, but stay true to the flow of the passage.

Verse 9 starts with the phrase "for this reason." What's the reason? Reread verses 3–8 and write down the reason Paul goes on to write the rest of this passage.

Today's text is a beautiful and powerful prayer that Paul prays for the Colossians and that believers have prayed for each other throughout the centuries. Let's dig into it a little more deeply. What does Paul specifically pray for? List out his requests in the space below.

As you read the passage again, circle the connecting phrases (e.g., "for this reason," "in order that," "so that"). How does each clause in this passage further explain or expound upon the preceding clause? (In other words, how does Paul drill deeper with each additional thought?)

The idea of fullness is a common theme in Colossians. Let's take a closer look at where Paul prays that God would fill the Colossians. Look up the word translated "fill" in the original Greek. What is the meaning of that verb?

Doing original word studies can be a lot of fun, but they can also be confusing, especially when you're just getting started, so we included some help for you in the Bible Study Quickstart Guide. Watch a video tutorial on how to do a word study at **myOneThingAlone.com/quickstart**.

According to Paul's prayer, what's the purpose of the knowledge of God (see v. 10)? How is spiritual knowledge different from just possessing facts? Check James 1:22–25 as a helpful cross-reference.)

Who accomplishes the work of sanctification in verses 6, 8, 9, and 11?

What role does the believer have in the process of sanctification described in Paul's prayer?

According to this passage, how do God's grace and believers' good works intersect daily life? (See also Ephesians 2:8–10 and James 2:14–26 for further clarification on this topic.)

ASSESS THE MAIN IDEA

Let's take a look at what other Christians throughout history have noticed in this text.

In his commentary on Colossians, church father Chrysostom notes that "with faith Paul always couples conduct" and Augustine comments on the importance of displaying our faithfulness through our living, stating, "As then we acknowledge the part played by the will when these commands are given, so let him acknowledge the part played by grace when these petitions are offered."[2] For even walking worthy of the Lord is made possible by God Himself, not by our own human will.

More recently, Bible scholars have noted the common themes of fullness and knowledge, both introduced here in verse 9:

> Paul used two key words, "fill" (*plēroō*) and "knowledge" (*epignōsis*, also used in v. 10 and 3:10). The first suggests a filling out to completeness, and the latter suggests a full, deep understanding. Such knowledge of God's will does not come from a fleshly mind (which "puffs up," 1 Cor. 8:1), but from the Holy Spirit who enlightens a believer's inner person (1 Cor. 2:5–6, 13), and from the Word of God. God's will, revealed in the Bible, is made known to believers by the Holy Spirit's teaching ministry. To this Paul added, **through all spiritual wisdom** (*sophia*; used six times in Col. 1:9, 28; 2:3, 23; 3:16; 4:5), that is, practical know-how which comes from God (James 1:5; 3:15), **and understanding** (*synesei*; also used in Col. 2:2), which speaks of clear analysis and decision-making in applying this knowledge to various problems. By contrast, the false teachers offered only "an appearance of wisdom" (*sophia*; 2:23), which captivated their minds and lives in legalistic regulations. But true spiritual wisdom is both stabilizing and liberating (Eph. 4:14). Knowledge (or understanding or intelligence) and wisdom are often connected in Scripture (cf. Ex. 31:3 ["skill" in the NIV is the Hebrew word for wisdom]; Deut. 4:6; Isa. 11:2; 1 Cor. 1:19). And the fear of the Lord is the beginning of both (cf. Prov. 1:7; 9:10).[3]

Using this insight, what did this passage mean to the original audience?

Write out the main idea of this passage in a single sentence. Make it precise, concise, and memorable. (Consider the following question to get you started: What does Jesus' grace accomplish in a believer's life?)

SPARK TRANSFORMATION

What comes to mind when you think of the word "theology"?

Theology is defined as the study of the nature of God. Would you consider yourself a theologian? Why or why not?

One of Paul's main themes in this letter is the transformational power of spiritual knowledge, specifically about God. And according to verse 12, God has "qualified you" to share in this knowledge of Him.

What's one specific way you can apply today's passage in your life to become a more confident theologian?

TURN TO GOD IN WORSHIP

Take a few moments to reflect on what this passage says about the character of God, then turn to Him in worship, praising Him for those attributes you see in the text and any other characteristics that come to mind.

WEEK 1 | DAY 5

SNACK ON THE GO

Read Colossians 1:12–14 out loud.

What is one thing you learn about God in this text? Write it in the space below.

How does this truth about God affect you? Your identity? Your worth? Your actions? Write down one specific application to your life today.

Write a short prayer, responding to God's Word to you today.

FEAST AT THE TABLE

FOCUS ON GOD

Open your Bible to Psalm 119:18. Write it out as a prayer to the Lord as you begin your study of His Word today.

ENGAGE THE TEXT

Read Colossians 1:12–14 out loud, then write it in the space below.

Write out whatever immediately jumps out at you in this text.

How has the Father "qualified" believers for His holy inheritance?

What is the inheritance mentioned in this passage? Why does Paul call it an inheritance?

Paul uses light and darkness as powerful symbols in this passage.

What do they each signify?

In what other passages of Scripture do you recall this same imagery being used? You might check a concordance to jog your memory.

Why would Paul employ this symbolism here?

Throughout Scripture we read that God used various means to accomplish His work on earth—individuals, the godly, the ungodly, nations, angels. But when it came to the work of our eternal salvation, God did not entrust it to any of these.

According to this passage, who does the work of redemption?

How was this "rescue" from one kingdom to another accomplished? (Hint: read on through verses 15–23.)

ASSESS THE MAIN IDEA

In light of the heretical teachings facing the Colossian church (see this week's introduction), what was Paul trying to communicate to the Colossians in this passage?

SPARK TRANSFORMATION

Jesus Christ's grace meets us where we are but it doesn't leave us as we are. His Spirit continues to work out sanctification in our lives, and as we continue studying this letter, we'll see how God's grace transforms us.

In what ways can you open yourself to the Holy Spirit's transformative work in your life?

TURN TO GOD IN WORSHIP

This passage beautifully describes redemption, which is "the deliverance and freedom from the penalty of sin by the payment of a ransom, the substitutionary death of Christ."[4]

What does this passage teach us about God, both in our redemption and our sanctification?

Worship God for the finished work of Jesus on the cross and the work He continues to do through His Spirit in your life. Then take a few moments to simply be still in His presence, acknowledging that because of Jesus, we don't have to hustle to gain God's favor; we can rest in His finished work of redemption and ongoing work of sanctification. (If this is your first time trying to practice stillness, set a timer for two minutes and quiet your mind and heart. Simply enter God's presence and rest.)

See more practical suggestions for practicing stillness at
onethingalone.com/practice-stillness-in-gods-presence.

WEEKEND REFLECTION

What did you learn about God this week?

What did you learn about yourself?

In what way is Jesus inviting you to trust that He is enough?

What do you most want to say to God right now?

rejoicing in Christ

The Son is the image of the invisible God, the firstborn over all creation. **COLOSSIANS 1:15**

Who is Jesus? And what qualifies Him to be the only way into the mysteries of God?

Imagine yourself sitting in a lecture hall, facing a blank paper with those two questions. What would you write?

Now imagine yourself facing a tribunal filled with angry people, ready to condemn you to hard labor or a torturous death for your answers to those very questions. What would you say?

For many men and women throughout history, these two scenarios were not imaginary exercises but daily realities, as they faced ridicule and persecution for the sake of Jesus. My own parents and other family members suffered at the hands of Romanian communists solely for their audacious commitment to Christ as Lord over all, over a political party or patriotism. Yet they would be the first to claim, along with hundreds of thousands around the world and even the apostle Paul himself, that they count it all joy to suffer for Jesus.

Because Jesus is worth it all.

You may not have faced that kind of intense scrutiny for your beliefs, and yet understanding who Jesus is and what qualifies Him to be the One we live and die for is at the very foundation of our Christian beliefs. This week we're going to study a church hymn that may have been in circulation at the time of Paul's letter to the Colossians, and see just how understanding who Jesus is leads to a life of rejoicing and adoration.

We can rejoice in who Jesus is, and we can rejoice in suffering for Him too, because we know that He is worthy.

The SON is the image of the invisible GOD, the firstborn over all creation.

COLOSSIANS 1:15

WEEK 2 | DAY 1

SNACK ON THE GO

Read Colossians 1:15–20.

When I was a teenager, I cautiously prayed to see God appear before me in physical form. I figured if I could just see Him, I'd never doubt that He was real.

In His wisdom, God didn't answer that prayer, but really, this request is nothing new. For thousands of years, people have wanted to see God. But the irony is that He's already revealed Himself.

In the space below, write out Colossians 1:15.

Have you ever wished to see and touch Jesus? Have you ever secretly thought that just a quick glimpse would be enough to seal your faith?

The truth is that even when Jesus walked the earth, people saw Him and still didn't believe. Even one of His disciples asked Him to show them God the Father. Jesus responded, "Anyone who has seen me has seen the Father" (John 14:9). Jesus is enough.

He is the image of the invisible God, and all the Father's powers and attributes dwell in Him. In Jesus, God fully revealed Himself to men and women (John 1:14, 18).

Sure, it would have been nice to have lived in Israel two thousand years ago, have seen Jesus teach and heal, and to have touched Him with our own hands. But Jesus said we're more blessed when we believe in Him without seeing Him (John 20:29).

We have all we need in the pages of Scripture. As twenty-first-century believers, we can learn to see and savor Jesus Christ as we study the Bible and as God's Holy Spirit awakens us to His presence.

What is one way you can make the most of this generous gift—Christ—revealed in Scripture? Write out a prayer asking the Father to help you know and love Him more as you learn about Jesus in the pages of your Bible.

FEAST AT THE TABLE

FOCUS ON GOD

Open your Bible to Psalm 119:27. Write out this verse as a prayer to the Lord as you begin your study of His Word today.

Today we get a special treat: we get to gaze into the beauty of Jesus. Begin by asking God to focus your heart and mind on Him and to awaken you to the exceeding brilliance of Jesus in this passage. Ask Him to move you not only on an intellectual level, but on an emotional and spiritual level as well, leading you into worshipful adoration as you study.

ENGAGE THE TEXT

Read Colossians 1:15–23 out loud, then write it in the space below.

As we're reading, we'll also keep a running list of all the attributes of Jesus we discover in this passage. And honestly, we could spend an entire day on each of these attributes, so feel free to go deeper on whichever ones you'd like if you have the time. There is such richness to the character and attributes of Jesus that we could never plumb His depths!

Verse 15 (ESV) says, "He is the image of the invisible God." Who is the "He" in this verse, according to verse 13b? Write down the exact term Paul uses.

Already, what does this tell us about Jesus? Where else can you think of in Scripture that uses this term for Jesus?

In verse 15, Jesus is described as "the image of the invisible God." What does this say about God (check John 1:18 as a helpful cross-reference)?

What does this say about Jesus (see John 1:18; 14:6–11; 2 Cor. 4:4; and Heb. 1:3)? What does it mean that he is God's "image"? (Your translation might also use words such as representation or imprint.)

Your Bible may have tiny letters or numbers written in the superscript of keywords and a listing of corresponding letters and verses in the center column or at the bottom of the page. These are referred to as "cross-references" and are typically other Bible verses that help explain the current verse either by providing more background, context, or another connection. To study a cross-reference, simply look up the corresponding letters and verses for the keyword you may be interested in, and write down additional observations based on that cross-reference. If your Bible does not have cross-references listed, you can use an online tool like **biblegateway.com** or **blueletterbible.com**.

Continue reading through Colossians 1:15–23, listing each attribute of Christ and, if you like, writing down observations based on each, either from this passage or from cross-references that you look up.

For example, looking at verse 13 we may notice that Jesus is "the Son he [God] loves":

> He is very God of very God; He is God's Son, in whom the Father is well-pleased; He is dearly loved with an eternal limitless love because God Himself is love; His very life is defined as sacrificial love, even from His purpose coming into the world (see John 3:16).

What role did Jesus play in the creation of the world, according to verses 16–17?

What does it mean that Jesus is the "firstborn over all creation"? If you have time, check out commentaries to find various interpretations. You might be surprised at what a rich discussion can originate from a singular phrase.

How many times does the phrase "all" or "everything" appear in this passage? What is Paul stressing through this repetition?

How does Colossians 2:9 further clarify this passage?

What else stands out to you in this passage?

ASSESS THE MAIN IDEA

Let's take a look at some commentaries:

> "The Greek word for *firstborn* can refer to one who was born first chronologically, but most often refers to preeminence in position, or rank. In both Greek and Jewish culture, the firstborn was the ranking son who had received the right of inheritance from his father, whether he was born first or not. It is used of Israel who, not being the first nation, was however the preeminent nation (cf. Ex. 4:22; Jer 31:9). *Firstborn* in this context clearly means highest in rank, not first created (cf. Ps. 89:27; Rev. 1:5)."[5]

"Consider the following words also: 'In our image' [Gen 1:26]. What do you say to this? Surely, the image of God and of the angels is not the same. Now it is absolutely necessary for the form of the Son and of the Father to be the same, the form being understood, of course, as becomes the divine, not in a bodily shape, but in the special properties of the Godhead. . . . To whom does he say: 'In our image'? To whom else, I say, than to the 'brightness of his glory and the image of his substance,' who is 'the image of the invisible God'?"[6]

"Please note that the same Moses says in another passage that God appeared to Abraham [Gen 12:7, 18:1]. Yet the same Moses hears from God that no man can see God and live [Exodus 33:20]. If God cannot be seen, how did God appear? If he appeared, how is it that he cannot be seen? . . . This can only mean that it was not the Father, who never has been seen, that was seen, but the Son, who is apt both to descend and to be seen, for the simple reason that he has descended. In fact, he is 'the image of the invisible God,' that our limited human nature and frailty might in time grow accustomed to see God the Father in him who is the Image of God, that is, in the Son of God."[7]

Summarize your main takeaways from these commentaries in the space below:

Write out the main idea of this passage in a single sentence. Make it precise, concise, and memorable. (Consider the following question: What are the implications of the fullness of God dwelling in Jesus as seen in this passage?)

SPARK TRANSFORMATION

Verses 15–20 are believed to be an early Christian hymn, expressing some of the most central doctrines to the Christian faith.[8] As you're thinking how the main idea applies to your life, consider this: Given that Jesus is the image of the invisible God and the totality of God, including all His powers and attributes, dwells in Him, what implications does that have for how Christians are to grow in the knowledge of God (as Paul prays in the preceding passage)?

What role does theology (i.e., Greek for "the study of the nature of God") play in the life of a typical woman today?

How can YOU grow in deeper knowledge of God? (A helpful resource you may want to check out is *The Knowledge of the Holy* by A. W. Tozer.)

TURN TO GOD IN WORSHIP

Today's passage is rich with reasons to worship God. Read through these verses out loud, turning your eyes, your hands, your mind, and your heart to God, and if you're musically inclined, feel free to make up music as you go. Then take a few moments to turn over to Him any situation in your life that is causing you to doubt His sufficiency. Declare over that situation and over your life that God is faithful to His promises and to His character, and that He is enough.

WEEK 2 | DAY 2

SNACK ON THE GO

"I once was lost, but now am found;
Was blind but now I see."

These familiar words of the hymn "Amazing Grace" demonstrate a powerful contrast between life before Christ and after Christ. Paul does something very similar in today's passage.

Read Colossians 1:21–23, and in the space below, write down three things that were true of the Colossians before Christ and three afterward.

As you reflect on your own life, what three words would you use to describe your life without Jesus?

Based on today's passage, how does Jesus change those words?

Today, praise Jesus because His "grace hath brought me safe thus far, and grace will lead me home."

FEAST AT THE TABLE

FOCUS ON GOD

Open your Bible to Psalm 119:33. Write it out as a prayer to the Lord as you begin your study of His Word today.

ENGAGE THE TEXT

Read Colossians 1:21–23 out loud, then write it in the space below.

This passage contrasts believers' former lives of sinfulness and condemnation with our glorious new status in Christ. Though modern translations break it up into more than one sentence, in the Greek we have one long sentence, whose main verb is a form of "reconcile." Look back at the preceding hymn, ending in verse 20. What is the main verb in verse 20?

How does today's passage relate to 1:15–20?

To help you understand this powerful contrast, let's sketch it out below. On the left, list everything that was "once" true about the Colossian believers (v. 21).

Now draw a vertical line above, and on the right list everything that is "now" true about them (v. 22). For a parallel passage, read Ephesians 5:25b–27, and Ephesians 1:4; according to these two passages, what is the purpose of God's reconciling work?

According to 22a, what caused the transformation from the left-hand column to the right-hand column?

Draw a horizontal line through your vertical line above to signify the cross, a symbol of Christ's suffering.

Take a closer look at verse 23. What word does it begin with? What does this signify? Remember that Paul wrote this letter to encourage the church in Colossae to resist false teachers and continue to grow in knowledge of Christ. How do God's reconciliation and human responsibility connect?

How may the Colossians continue in their faith? How does this contrast with false teachers who were trying to sway the Colossians from their faith?

Does this warning imply that Paul is uncertain? Or confident? Peek ahead at 2:5. How does Paul's statement about the Colossians' faith help clarify his meaning here?

What three things does Paul say about the gospel at the end of verse 23?

Based on these three observations, what is "the hope held out in the gospel" at the beginning of verse 23? (See also Col. 1:5–6, Titus 1:2, and 1 Peter 1:4.)

How does this passage pick up on the theme in verses 12–14?

What else stands out to you in this passage?

ASSESS THE MAIN IDEA

Write out the main idea of this passage in a single sentence. Make it precise, concise, and memorable.

Need extra help with assessing the main idea? You might find it helpful to watch the video tutorial on how to interpret a Bible text—included in the Bible Study Quickstart Guide—at **myOneThingAlone.com/quickstart**.

SPARK TRANSFORMATION

Look at the chart you drew on the other page. As you look at the two columns, which one do you most identify with?

The enemy has a sneaky way of making us feel alienated from God, as if we were still His enemies, reminding us of all our evil behavior. But if we take God at His Word, we can be confident that Jesus Christ secured for us another reality altogether.

What are the "evil behaviors" of your past that keep coming to mind? What things make you feel far from God still? What parts of your past continue to haunt you? List them in the space below, and then surrender them to God in prayer. Draw the cross of Jesus, signifying His death and payment for all your sins, and then write out what is true about you in Christ Jesus, claiming each truth as applying to you personally, right here and right now.

In the days and weeks to come, when Satan "tempts you to despair and tells you of the guilt within," look to the One "who made an end to all your sins," and praise Him for reconciling you to Himself. These words are from the hymn "Before the Throne of God Above" written in 1863 by Charitie Lees Smith.

TURN TO GOD IN WORSHIP

Our hymnals are filled with beautiful songs that recount the transformation Jesus Christ caused in us, through His death on the cross. Today, end your time FEAST-ing on God's Word by singing one of these songs to Him. "Before the Throne of God Above" is one of my favorites, but whichever one you choose, allow your soul to lift up to heaven with thanksgiving and praise.

WEEK 2 | DAY 3

SNACK ON THE GO

Right now, somewhere in the world, a brother or sister in Christ is suffering.

Persecution for Christ's name is a daily reality for thousands of Christians around the world. And it's nothing new. If anything, it's normal. It's expected. Jesus told His disciples to expect to suffer for following Him, and Paul experienced this very thing as well.

Open your Bible to Colossians 1:24, and write this verse in the space below.

Paul suffered afflictions because he preached the good news that Jesus' sacrifice is enough for our atonement with God, and for thousands of years Christians continue to do the same.

Do you wonder how you can partner with those suffering for the sake of the gospel?

Pray.

Pray not necessarily that God would end their persecution, but rather that God would empower them to stand firm in the midst of intense suffering. Pray that God would use their witness to bring their persecutors to believe in Jesus Christ. Pray that their hearts would be encouraged and their faith would be bolstered. Pray that God would provide for their physical needs. Pray that their children and spouses would stay close to Christ. Pray that they would be filled with joy. And pray that you also may learn from their example.

Write a simple prayer for the persecuted church in the space below.

For more information on how to pray for the persecuted church, go to persecution.com.

FEAST AT THE TABLE

FOCUS ON GOD

Open your Bible to Psalm 119:37. Write it out as a prayer to the Lord as you begin your study of His Word today.

ENGAGE THE TEXT

Read Colossians 1:24 out loud and then write it in the space below.

Today we're focusing on just one verse because there's so much packed in here and also because, if you're like many Bible readers throughout history, it probably made you pause and go, "huh?" It's okay to have questions. Sometimes questions are what lead to the most fascinating discoveries. So let's dig in.

Write down any immediate observations that come to mind, as well as any questions you may have about Colossians 1:24.

What had Paul suffered for the Colossians, either directly or in his preaching of the gospel to the Gentiles? Read through the following accounts, and note below what Paul had suffered physically, emotionally/relationally, mentally, spiritually:

ACTS 16:16–24

1 CORINTHIANS 4:9–13

2 CORINTHIANS 4:8–9

2 CORINTHIANS 6:3–13

2 CORINTHIANS 7:5

2 CORINTHIANS 11:23–33

Let's get to the main tension in Colossians 1:24: What does Paul mean when he says he's filling up "what is still lacking in regard to Christ's afflictions"? Is Paul saying there's a deficiency in the atoning sacrifice of Christ? If not, what is he getting at? And how do his sufferings benefit the worldwide church? These questions exemplify how important it is to allow Scripture to interpret Scripture; in other words, as good students of Scripture, we should not extrapolate what we *think* Paul might mean here—we must dig deep into the text and cross-texts, as well as Jewish literature that would have been familiar to Paul and his readers, in order to understand this discussion in its proper context. So let's take a closer look.

Is Jesus Christ's sacrifice enough to accomplish the redemption of His people? (See Colossians 1:19–20 and 2:13–15 in this letter alone, and feel free to pursue other cross-references as well.)

Read John 15:18–25. What does Jesus say about the presence of suffering in believers' lives?

How did Jesus frame this issue with Paul himself, who before his conversion was ravaging the church (Acts 9:1–5)? Who did Jesus say Paul/Saul was persecuting?

How does Revelation 6:9–11 add to your understanding of "filling up" the tribulations that are inevitably a part of the last days as believers await Jesus' return?

How did Paul's afflictions, which you noted earlier, affect the Colossian church specifically?

What else stands out to you as you read these passages on suffering?

ASSESS THE MAIN IDEA

Whoa. That was a lot to study on just one verse, and you may still have some unanswered questions. That's okay. This is a good place to pull out some commentaries to help you interpret this verse correctly.

Here's one excerpt that may help:

Paul rejoiced that he was able to suffer for them what was still lacking in regard to Christ's afflictions. By this he did not mean that Christ's suffering on the cross was insufficient (cf. Rom. 3:21–26; Heb. 10:10–14). He was speaking not of salvation but of service. Christ's suffering alone procures salvation (1 Peter 1:11; 5:1; Heb. 2:9). But it is a believer's privilege to suffer for Christ (2 Tim. 3:11; 1 Peter 3:13–14; 5:9; Heb. 10:32). The word "affliction" (*thlipsis*)—never used in the New Testament of Christ's death—means "distress," "pressure," or "trouble" (which Paul had plenty of; 2 Cor. 11:23–29). Ordinarily it refers to trials in life, not the pains of death. Christ does indeed continue to suffer when Christians suffer for Him. He asked Saul (later called Paul) on the Damascus Road, "Why do you persecute Me?" (Acts 9:4). Since the church is Christ's body, He is affected when it is affected. For the sake of Christ's body Paul willingly suffered (Phil. 1:29).[9]

Let's take a step back to look at the big picture. What did this verse mean to the original audience?

Write out the main idea of this passage in a single sentence. Make it precise, concise, and memorable. (Consider the following question: How do Paul's tribulations build up the local church in Colossae and the worldwide missionary work among the Gentiles?)

SPARK TRANSFORMATION

The idea of suffering for the sake of the gospel can make us a little uncomfortable. We might admire others who have suffered for Christ's sake, but us? If we're honest, most of us would rather be safe. Comfortable. Happy. Prosperous. Respected. Admired.

But, as John Piper points out in his book on global missions *Let the Nations Be*

Glad, the relative absence of persecution enjoyed by most of the Western church today is abnormal in the context of the past two thousand years of church history. Jesus tells us to expect to suffer for the sake of the gospel. Persecution is the norm. Freedom of religion is the exception.

While many of us today may enjoy freedom from religious persecution, we must prepare ourselves for the eventuality of suffering for the gospel of Jesus, not in fear and anxiety, but in steadfastness and perseverance. It's important to note this: *it's not a matter of whether or not we will experience persecution, but rather a matter of how we can prepare now to stand steadfast when it comes.*

This is a heavy topic, and perhaps your heart seems burdened right now. Take some time to talk with the Lord about your fears, your reactions, and your trepidations. What do you want to say to Him?

How might He be asking you to prepare here and now to face future opposition?

Some ideas you may consider:

- Memorize Scripture. Lots of it. The time may come when your Bible is taken away, but no one can steal God's Word that you've hidden in your heart.

- Set aside a day each week to fast and pray, asking God to tear down idols that compete for your affection and help you watch for and anticipate Jesus' return.

- Read biographies of men and women throughout history who have suffered for Christ's sake.

- Subscribe to Voice of the Martyrs (at persecution.com) to educate yourself about persecution around the world and intercede for your brothers and sisters in Christ who are suffering.

- Pray that God would give you His perspective on suffering for His sake (Acts 5:41; Phil. 3:10–11).

To learn more about Christians who have endured hardships for Christ's sake, visit **OneThingAlone.com/christian-biographies**.

TURN TO GOD IN WORSHIP

It is because of Jesus Christ's finished work on the cross that we have the privilege of joining Him in suffering for His sake, of knowing the "power of his resurrection and participation in his sufferings" (Phil. 3:10). And all of our suffering? It's for Him. Because He is worthy.

Turn a few pages in your Bible to Revelation 7:9–17 to get a glimpse of how all this suffering ends. Allow the words to lift off the page and lift your soul to God in worship. Praise Him that because of Jesus, we can face the unknown future with joy and peace instead of fear and trepidation.

WEEK 2 | DAY 4

SNACK ON THE GO

"Let me tell you a secret."

Who doesn't love hearing those words? From surprise birthday parties to mystery novels, we all love a good secret, especially when we get to find out the hidden nugget before others do.

As twenty-first-century Christians, we get this privilege, because God reveals a centuries-old mystery to us in Scripture.

Read Colossians 1:24–27, and write verse 27 below.

According to this verse, what is the mystery that is now revealed?

How does this impact your life today?

FEAST AT THE TABLE

FOCUS ON GOD

Open your Bible to Psalm 119:40–41. Write out these verses as a prayer to the Lord as you begin your study of His Word today.

ENGAGE THE TEXT

Read Colossians 1:24–27 out loud and then write it in the space below.

Write down your immediate observations.

Yesterday we looked at verse 24 in depth, and today we'll use what we've learned to study the verses that follow in context. Remember that this young church was facing considerable challenges from heretical teachers who claimed to have exclusive access to secret knowledge, mysteries about the spiritual realm available to only the select few.

Peek ahead to Colossians 1:28–2:3 and underline each variation of the words "knowledge," "wisdom," and any synonyms. How does Paul play with this language to reveal the real mystery of the gospel?

Reread verses 26–27 out loud. Can you sense the anticipation Paul is building up as he talks about the mystery of the gospel? List below the ways he describes this mystery.

What do each of these phrases add to our comprehension of this mystery?

At the end of verse 27, Paul finally reveals this mystery. What aspects of God's work are included in this mystery?

Why is this a mystery?

Let's take a closer look at the glorious riches of this mystery, as Paul presents it in various letters. Look up each of the following cross-references, and briefly note what each says on this topic:

ROMANS 2:4

ROMANS 9:23–24

EPHESIANS 1:7–10

EPHESIANS 1:17–19

EPHESIANS 2:6–7

EPHESIANS 3:7–10

EPHESIANS 3:16-17

COLOSSIANS 2:2-3

Whereas in other passages Paul's emphasis regarding this mystery is this signifi-cant historical shift to include Gentiles into the salvation plan that was previously available only to Jews, Paul here keeps his emphasis on Christ. It's all about Jesus, and even though the other aspects are true, the Colossians needed to be reminded most that the mystery is "Christ in you" (Col. 1:27).

What does the phrase "Christ in you" mean?

In what ways does Jesus Christ inhabit those He has redeemed? (For help on inter-preting this phrase, check out the related cross-references: Rom. 8:10; 2 Cor. 13:5; Gal. 2:20, 4:19; and Eph. 3:17.)

How does the hope Paul refers to here relate to the hope he describes in the open-ing of his letter, in Colossians 1:5 and 1:23?

What else stands out to you in this passage?

ASSESS THE MAIN IDEA

Write out the main idea of this passage in a single sentence. Make it precise, concise, and memorable. (Consider the following question: What are the riches of the mystery of God revealed in Jesus Christ?)

SPARK TRANSFORMATION

As you consider the main idea you've written above, ask the Holy Spirit to help you see how this impacts your life. Ask Him, "How should I respond?" This may be an attribute of God to worship, a sin to confess, a lie to replace with truth, a habit to surrender, an action to adopt, or something completely different. Allow the Holy Spirit to lead you in your own personal application of the text, and ask Him to spark transformation in your heart and life.

TURN TO GOD IN WORSHIP

What a privilege! To be among those who know and understand this "mystery that [had] been kept hidden for ages and generations!" And not only to know, but to be included among those who have Christ in them! What grace! What mercy! What love!

Spend some time responding to the riches of God's love, worshiping Him for who He is and thanking Him for choosing you. Feel free to write out a prayer of thanks or listen to your favorite worship music related to His deep love.

WEEK 2 | DAY 5

SNACK ON THE GO

As a mom to two young girls, I know what it's like to stay up with a baby all night only to be pulled in all directions by a toddler in the morning. And while motherhood is hard, you don't have to be a mom to feel exhausted and perpetually behind. Whether you're a college student, career woman, mom, grandma, or anything in between, you probably know what early mornings and late nights feel like. And you might just have a love affair with coffee to keep you sane.

While in different circumstances, Paul understood what it was like to struggle. He was beaten, stoned, shackled in a cold cell, left to starve, shipwrecked, and betrayed by his own people. And yet Paul continued to spread the gospel, despite all his hardships. His secret?

> I strenuously contend with all the energy Christ so powerfully works in me. **COLOSSIANS 1:29**

Whose energy is that? Jesus Christ's. This is one of my favorite motherhood verses, because it reminds me that the Spirit of Jesus Christ is alive in me, and when I am weak I can lean into His energy to work powerfully in me. Next time you feel like you're at the end of your wits, ask God to infuse you with His energy, and then watch Him work.

Today, consider writing out this verse (Col. 1:29) on a sticky note and posting it somewhere you'll see it often to be reminded of this truth.

FEAST AT THE TABLE

FOCUS ON GOD

Open your Bible to Psalm 119:47–48. Write it out as a prayer to the Lord as you begin your study of His Word today.

ENGAGE THE TEXT

Read Colossians 1:24–2:5 out loud and write the passage in the space below.

Write down your immediate observations.

Today we continue to build on what we've already learned about this passage, but we'll be focusing on the first part of chapter 2. Before we begin, review the main ideas you've written out for each of the passages you've studied this week and distill it all into one summary statement below:

Now let's dig in. Based on 1:28, what or who is the focus of Paul's preaching and teaching?

Why is this significant, in light of what we've studied this past week?

Paul has already established himself as a servant of the gospel. But how does he labor, according to verse 29?

What implications does this have for the work of the gospel?

How does this verse explain the work of the gospel that Paul describes in chapter 1?

What is Paul's goal, according to 2:2?

How does this relate to his prayer in 1:9–11?

Paul is deliberate in this letter to keep pointing these new believers back to Jesus, and this is evident in today's passage as well. As you reread today's passage (Col. 1:24–2:5), highlight every reference to Jesus, directly or indirectly, and briefly describe what each reference reveals about Jesus.

Whereas the false teachers taught that the mysteries of spiritual knowledge were available to only a select few, Paul taught something completely different. As you reread the passage, circle the words "all," "everyone," and "full."

What is Paul communicating here about the sufficiency of Christ and who this knowledge is available to?

Why is this significant?

What else stands out to you in this passage?

ASSESS THE MAIN IDEA

What did this text mean to the original audience?

Write out the main idea of this passage in a single sentence. Make it precise, concise, and memorable. (Consider the following question: What does this passage say about the universality of the gospel and the exclusiveness of Christ?)

SPARK TRANSFORMATION

How does what you studied today apply to your life? Make it a SMART application: specific, measurable, attainable, realistic, and time-bound.

TURN TO GOD IN WORSHIP

Take a moment to look back on what you learned in Colossians 1. What are some things that stood out to you?

Today, purposefully engage your right brain in creative worship. Paint a picture of your response to Jesus when you read 1:15–20. Sing theologically rich songs that make your heart soar. Put on some praise music and dance before the Lord. Go on a prayer hike, praising Jesus for His creativity in designing the beautiful world all around you, from the most intricate pattern on a leaf or snowflake to the gorgeous sunsets in the sky.

For more creative worship ideas, including video tutorials and a fun Worship Personality quiz, find our Jumpstart Your Creative Worship Experience at **myOneThingAlone.com/jumpstart-creative-worship.**

WEEKEND REFLECTION

What did you learn about God this week?

What did you learn about yourself?

In what way is Jesus inviting you to trust that He is enough?

What do you most want to say to God right now?

complete in Christ

For in Christ all the fullness of the Deity lives in bodily form, and in Christ you have been brought to fullness.

COLOSSIANS 2:9–10a

What do you want most of all?

Perhaps you have a wish list of things you'd like to own. Or maybe a bucket list of things you'd like to experience or goals to achieve.

We all live yearning for the next thing. Whether it's as trivial as trying the newest food trend or as spiritual as reading the Bible through in a year (finally!), we all yearn for the next big thing. But even more important than checking that "thing" off our list is considering how we're going to get there.

For the first-century believers in Colossae, one of the major things on their list was spiritual union with God. They wanted to be right with God, and there was no shortage of people willing to tell them exactly how they could do that. Some argued for religious observances like circumcision, holy days, and rules about food. Others suggested angel worship and secret rituals and other mystical practices.

It's tempting to hold on to a checklist of things to do, because that gives us the illusion of being in control. But Paul speaks firmly against these teachings, explaining that those who promote such philosophies and legalism are not holding on to

Jesus. It's Christ alone, he says, and He is enough. Watch out for anyone who tries to tell you otherwise.

In fact, in one of my favorite passages in the whole book, Paul states that all the fullness of the deity dwells in Jesus in bodily form, and we have been brought to that fullness through Jesus. United with Him, we are complete, and that reality leads to a thriving life both here and now and in the age to come.

For in Christ
all the FULLNESS
of the Deity
LIVES IN BODILY FORM,
and in Christ
YOU HAVE BEEN BROUGHT
to fullness.

COLOSSIANS 2:9-10a

WEEK 3 | DAY 1

SNACK ON THE GO

This week's passage is the heart of Paul's letter to these new believers. Everything he's written up to this point builds the foundation for these verses, and everything that follows unpacks the practical implications of this message.

Open your Bible to Colossians 2:6–7, and write out the verses in the space below.

There's such rich imagery here, and so much to meditate on. So that's my encouragement to you this week: as you go through your busy days, keep coming back to these two verses, something to snack on in the midst of the busyness. Spend one minute each morning and evening reading these verses out loud. Consider making up hand motions to go with the verses, and use them as if you were teaching the passage to a young child. It might feel silly at first, but you may be surprised how much hand gestures will help you remember the words.

Whenever you recite these verses, ask the Holy Spirit to help you understand them, to recognize the beauty of Jesus Christ in them, and to shape your life as you meditate on them. Because even as you do this, you will be living out the meaning of these verses.

FEAST AT THE TABLE

FOCUS ON GOD

Open your Bible to Psalm 119:54. Write it out as a prayer to the Lord as you begin your study of His Word today.

ENGAGE THE TEXT

Read Colossians 2:6–7 out loud.

Write down your immediate observations.

Today's passage begins with the phrase "so then," which indicates a shift or transition in thought, building on the argument already made. Review chapter 1 of Colossians to familiarize yourself with the context, and summarize the main point in the space below (you might want to check your notes from last week).

Map out today's passage. Begin with the main clause, "continue to live your lives in him," and map out the rest of the passage around the main idea. Don't stress about getting it grammatically right—focus instead on how the ideas in this passage relate to each other.

Interestingly, Paul uses his introductory prayer in 1:10–12 to set up important themes that he develops later in the letter (here and in the following chapters).

How is this passage similar to that prayer?

What themes surface as you look at the two passages side by side?

Take a look at the first phrase, "just as you received Christ Jesus as Lord." Based on what you've already studied in chapter 1 and the first few verses of chapter 2, what stands out to you in this phrase?

What does the term "received" indicate?

What have we already learned about the significance of Jesus' lordship?

What do the names "Christ" and "Jesus" each signify? (Check a Bible dictionary or commentary if you're unsure.)

Let's move to the phrase "continue to live your lives in him." What does "continue" indicate?

Using an online Bible dictionary, look up the Greek word translated "live." What does it mean?

How is this significant?

What about the phrase "in him"—who does it refer to? This phrase sets the stage for a deeper discussion of this idea in the next passage (2:7–11), and we'll study it more closely in the following days.

In verse 7, Paul uses four phrases to describe the nature of living in Christ. List them below, and explain what each states about the Christian life.

What else stands out to you in this passage?

ASSESS THE MAIN IDEA

What did these verses mean to the original audience?

Write out the main idea of this passage in a single sentence. Make it precise, concise, and memorable.

SPARK TRANSFORMATION

This passage is a beautiful description of what our life in Christ looks like. As you reflect on your own life, in what ways is it similar to this passage and how is it different?

Spend some time responding to God today, perhaps focusing on one particular aspect of your life in Christ, and ask Him to show you how to continue to live your life in Him. If the Spirit prompts, consider making your application SMART using the guidelines below:

SPECIFIC:

MEASURABLE:

ATTAINABLE:

REALISTIC:

TIME-BOUND:

TURN TO GOD IN WORSHIP

Once again, Paul reminds us in this passage that it's all about Jesus. Our salvation begins and ends with Him, and even our daily walk with God is dependent on Him.

As you end your study time, consider picking up some crayons or paint brushes and sketch out what life in Christ looks like. Allow your illustration to guide you in prayer, worshiping the God who would choose you, dwell in you, empower you, root you, build you, strengthen you, and fill you with Himself.

WEEK 3 | DAY 2

SNACK ON THE GO

Do you live in the land of "if only"?

If only I lost ten pounds . . . If only I had a bigger house . . . If only my children obeyed . . . If only my husband were more spiritual . . . If only I got a raise . . . If only . . .

What's your "if only"? What's the script that runs through your mind, that makes you think you're *this close* to real happiness, if only those remaining pieces fell into place? Write yours below:

It's tempting to think that fulfillment is just beyond our reach, if only we stretched our arm out a little farther, but Scripture tells us that the fullness of life is already ours in Jesus Christ, if only we recognize and receive it:

> For in Christ all the fullness of the Deity lives in bodily form, and in Christ you have been brought to fullness. He is the head over every power and authority. COLOSSIANS 2:9-10

Did you catch that? You've been brought to fullness in Christ. There is no other "if only" that will fulfill you. Losing that weight, getting that paycheck, moving into that neighborhood . . . all these things may make you feel better in the moment, but they don't bring lasting satisfaction because they were never meant to. The full life is not beyond our reach; it's already ours in Christ Jesus when we find our satisfaction in Him.

Today, consider what "if onlys" you've bought into, and replace those lies with the truth that Jesus has already given you the fullness of life in Him. Rewrite your "if only" with what is true about Jesus (who He is) and how that transforms this area of your life (who you are).

FEAST AT THE TABLE

FOCUS ON GOD

Open your Bible to Psalm 119:55–56. Write it out as a prayer to the Lord as you begin your study of His Word today.

ENGAGE THE TEXT

Read Colossians 2:8–15 out loud; then write it in the space below.

Write down your observations after reading through the text.

As we learned last week, Paul was writing to a specific audience with specific considerations in mind, one of which was to address heresy that had infiltrated the young church. These false teachers "taught that for salvation one needed to combine faith in Christ with secret knowledge and with man-made regulations concerning such physical and external practices as circumcision, eating and drinking, and observance of religious festivals."[10]

According to verse 8 and 1 Timothy 6:20–21, what was attractive about this teaching?

In what ways did this teaching minimize the sacrifice of Jesus Christ?

What does Jesus have that He has also given to believers (see vv. 9–10)?

In your own words, define what the word "fullness" means. Look up the meaning of the original Greek word using an online dictionary.

Look up the cross-references for the word in John 10:10 and Ephesians 3:19, and add how these passages enhance your understanding of the word.

What else stands out to you?

ASSESS THE MAIN IDEA

What did this mean to the original audience?

Write out the main idea of this passage in a single sentence. Make it precise, concise, and memorable. Remember to keep your interpretation limited to the text: there and then. We'll bring it to here and now in the application step.

SPARK TRANSFORMATION

Do you see yourself as being complete in Christ?

In what ways do you feel deficient?

What does Scripture say about your completeness in Christ?

How can you renew your mind with Scripture, so that when you're tempted to view yourself as "less than," you can fight that with the Truth of Scripture?

Make your application SMART: specific, measurable, attainable, realistic, and time-bound.

TURN TO GOD IN WORSHIP

Look up the lyrics to "Jesus, Lover of My Soul (It's All About You)" by Shelley Nirider recorded at Passion Conference, and allow the song to prompt your response to Jesus today.

WEEK 3 | DAY 3

SNACK ON THE GO

Today's passage, Colossians 2:11–15, is a beautiful portrayal of the gospel message, namely the way in which God made sinful humans holy and complete in Christ, demonstrating that Christ is enough.

Read the text in your Bible, and then read it again in a version that you're not as familiar with, perhaps the New Living Translation or The Message, and allow the beautiful imagery to sink deep into your heart. What's something that stands out to you as you read?

Throughout the day, reread this passage. Consider listening to it on your phone through a free app like YouVersion, or record yourself reading the passage, and listen to it over and over again.

These words are true of you, if you've received Jesus Christ as Lord. Allow them to reorient your heart in worship throughout your day.

FEAST AT THE TABLE

FOCUS ON GOD

Open your Bible to Psalm 119:57. Write it out as a prayer to the Lord as you begin your study of His Word today.

ENGAGE THE TEXT

Read Colossians 2:11–15 out loud and write the passage in the space below.

Write down your immediate observations.

Review 2:9–10. How did this teaching radically oppose the heresy facing the Colossian believers?

In the verses that follow, Paul unpacks exactly how believers in Christ were given of His fullness. Read verses 11–15 and list out what Jesus accomplished on the cross for all who believe in Him.

What do you know about the circumcision Paul references in verses 11 and 13?

How did reliance on this Jewish custom take away from the sufficiency of Jesus' redemptive work?

How do believers participate in Jesus Christ's burial and resurrection (vv. 12–13)? Who does the work in these verses?

What imagery does Paul use in verse 14?

How does this wording illustrate the spiritual truth of being forgiven in Christ?

According to verse 15, what did Jesus do on the cross? Why is this significant?

What else stands out to you in this passage?

ASSESS THE MAIN IDEA

In order to interpret the meaning of this passage, we must first understand the importance of circumcision to Old Testament Jews, and how this ritual caused dissension between Jewish and Gentile converts. Below is a brief description of the origin and controversy of circumcision:

> [Circumcision is the] act of removing the foreskin of the male genital. In ancient Israel this act was ritually performed on the eight day after birth upon children of natives, servants, and aliens (Gen. 17:12–14; Lev. 12:3). . . . In the OT the origin of Israelite practice was founded upon the circumcision of Abraham as a sign of the covenant between God and the patriarch (Gen. 17:10). . . .

Controversy arose in the early church (Acts 15:1–12) as to whether Gentile converts needed to be circumcised. First-century A.D. Jews disdained the uncircumcised. The leadership of the apostle Paul in the Jerusalem Council was crucial in the settlement of the dispute: circumcision was not essential to Christian faith and fellowship. Circumcision of the heart via repentance and faith were the only requirements (Rom. 4:9–12; Gal. 2:15–21).[11]

Having read the commentary above, describe the main tension in this passage. What would this text have meant to the original audience?

Write out the main idea of this passage in a single sentence. Make it precise, concise, and memorable. (Consider the following question: How do believers participate in the fullness of Jesus?)

SPARK TRANSFORMATION

The "charge of our legal indebtedness" in verse 14 was a business term that referred to a certificate of indebtedness, and here Paul applied it to demands of the Old Testament Law. Another version phrases it "record of debt that stood against us with its legal demands" (ESV).

Picture your own "record of debt"—what's written on it?

In what ways have you fallen short of God's standard of holiness and perfection?

So many of us carry an unwritten list in our hearts of all the ways we've failed. We might know in our minds that Jesus nailed our list to the cross, but we keep climbing up there, tearing it down, rolling it up, and carrying it around as if it's still ours. It's hard to believe we're really forgiven.

Now, using your sanctified imagination, picture God taking that list and nailing it to the cross, and giving you a certificate that states "paid in full." Allow this new image to burn in your heart and mind, replacing the old certificate of indebtedness. Hear Jesus' words, spoken over you: "It is finished." You're no longer a slave, no longer in debt, no longer in chains. He has taken all that away and nailed it to the cross, and in doing so, disarmed any foreign power or authority over you.

You are His. And He is yours. Celebrate that beautiful truth today.

TURN TO GOD IN WORSHIP

What does this passage say about God? His character? His choices? His love?

Allow the words of this classic hymn, written by Charles Wesley in 1738, to guide your heart in worship:

> And can it be that I should gain
> An interest in the Savior's blood?
> Died He for me, who caused His pain—
> For me, who Him to death pursued?
> Amazing love! How can it be,
> That Thou, my God, shouldst die for me?
> No condemnation now I dread;
> Jesus, and all in Him, is mine;
> Alive in Him, my living Head,
> And clothed in righteousness divine,
> Bold I approach the eternal throne,
> And claim the crown, through Christ my own.

WEEK 3 | DAY 4

SNACK ON THE GO

"Real Christians don't play cards."

If I heard it once, I heard it a hundred times growing up. My church community had come up with a list of dos and don'ts, and card-playing was most definitely a don't. Perhaps your community's list of dos and don'ts growing up was different than mine, and maybe you're still surrounded by people who judge your spirituality based on how well you follow their rules.

These lists are not a new phenomenon in Christianity; in fact, they were around from the very beginning of the church. But the problem with these lists is that they ignore the gospel.

Here's how Paul puts it:

> Since you died with Christ to the elemental spiritual forces of this world, why, as though you still belonged to the world, do you submit to its rules: 'Do not handle! Do not taste! Do not touch!'? These rules, which have to do with things that are all destined to perish with use, are based on merely human commands and teachings. **COLOSSIANS 2:20–21**

Paul actually goes on to call these rules "self-imposed worship" and "false humility," because they dismiss the finished work of Jesus Christ on the cross. Those of us who have died and been resurrected with Jesus are now free to live the full life that Jesus secured for us. Christ is enough, both for our salvation and our sanctification.

What's on your spiritual list of dos and don'ts? Which of these rules are "based on merely human commands and teachings"?

As you write down each item on your list, surrender it to God, thanking Him for setting you free from human regulations and rejoicing in the truth that Christ is enough.

FEAST AT THE TABLE

FOCUS ON GOD

Open your Bible to Psalm 119:58. Write it out as a prayer to the Lord as you begin your study of His Word today.

ENGAGE THE TEXT

Read Colossians 2:16–23 out loud—then write it in the space below.

Write down any observations that immediately stand out to you.

What additional details do we learn about the Colossian heresy based on this passage?

Paul describes the Old Testament regulations that false teachers held to as "a shadow of the things that were to come," which find their fulfillment in Jesus Christ. According to Hebrews 10:1–10, what was the purpose of these laws?

Paul talks here about "false humility" (Col. 2:23). In what ways did the false teachers' actions have an appearance of humility? What is true humility?

As you read verse 19, describe what it means that Jesus is the head. What are the implications of His headship?

How does humility relate to submitting to "the head"?

In what ways do external regulations fail to restrain sensual indulgence (see verse 23)? Another version puts it like this: "They provide no help in conquering a person's evil desires" (NLT).

According to this passage, how does true humility result in real life change?

What does this passage say about God's character?

ASSESS THE MAIN IDEA

Before you interpret the text, you might still have questions about one aspect of the Colossian heresy, namely, "What's with the worship of angels?" Take a look at this explanation of "worship of angels" taken from Douglas Moo's commentary on Colossians 2:18:

> A key concern of Colossians has been to accentuate the superiority of Christ over spiritual beings (1:16, 20; 2:10, 15). Such a concern to minimize the significance of the angels would make very good sense if, indeed, the false teachers were worshiping them. [New Testament scholar] Clinton Arnold has suggested a plausible background for Paul's accusation that the false teachers were worshiping angels. He notes the importance of invoking angels as a means to ward off evil in the ancient world in general and the geographic region of Colossae in particular. Paul would be characterizing this calling on angels for protection as tantamount to the worship of angels.[12]

How does this short commentary help you understand what this passage meant to the original audience?

Write out the main idea of this passage in a single sentence. Make it precise, concise, and memorable.

SPARK TRANSFORMATION

While few Christians feel burdened by Old Testament laws today, what "regulations" or "rules" do today's false teachers place on unsuspecting Christians' shoulders?

What kinds of activities do you feel like you have to do to be right with God? (e.g., tithing, volunteering, fasting . . . even studying the Bible or praying?)

How does today's central truth apply to your life?

What would it look like for you to live out what is already true about you in Christ, according to this passage?

TURN TO GOD IN WORSHIP

True humility is rooted in our awareness of God's greatness and our desperate neediness. Trying to gain God's approval by following human rules is actually mock humility—it's minimizing Jesus' sacrifice and declaring that what He did on the cross is not enough. Today, reflect on the truth that you desperately need Jesus and only Jesus. He is enough. He is enough. Say it aloud with me: He is enough. Respond to today's text with a prayer of confession expressing your neediness and Christ's sufficiency. Then worship Him for being enough through a song like "Christ Is Enough" by Hillsong.

WEEK 3 | DAY 5

SNACK ON THE GO

How are you doing with your memory verses?

Remember, there is no condemnation for us in Christ Jesus. But we have strong encouragement in Paul's letter to the Colossians to grow in our faith in Jesus and to stand firm in Him. So today, review your memory verses and reflect on what you've learned so far about Jesus.

Write out a prayer of worship and thanksgiving for who Jesus is and what He's doing in your life:

FEAST AT THE TABLE

Close studies of the text are fun, but so is zooming out and looking at the big picture. Today we'll set aside our magnifying glasses and pick up the binoculars to look at the text from a broader perspective.

FOCUS ON GOD

Open your Bible to Psalm 119:64. Write it out as a prayer to the Lord as you begin your study of His Word today.

ENGAGE THE TEXT

Reread Colossians, from start to finish. Remember it only takes about fifteen minutes. As you read, underline any reference to Jesus (whether directly by name or pronoun, like "He" or "Him"), circle the phrase "in Christ/Him" and draw a rectangle around the phrase "with Christ/Him." (You may print out the book of Colossians and do this exercise on copy paper if you'd rather not draw in your Bible.)

Look back at your markings. What patterns do you notice?

How does it illustrate the sufficiency of Christ?

Summarize the main point of Colossians 1–2.

The end of Colossians 2 marks a definitive shift in Paul's focus in this letter as he moves into a more pastoral tone. As we prepare to dive into the second half of the book, let's take a look at the references to Jesus in chapter 3. How does Paul refer to Jesus? What title does he predominantly use?

Let's pause to define our terms. Using a Bible dictionary, look up the meaning of one or two names or titles of Jesus that appear in Colossians.

Is the title Paul uses in chapter 3 for Jesus similar to or different from how he refers to Him in chapters 1–2? Why would that be, especially considering the context of 3:18–25?

What new title appears in 4:1? Does this title appear anywhere else in the letter? What is its significance at the end of Paul's instructions in 3:18–25?

Besides references to Jesus, what other persons of the Godhead does Paul talk about?

In the space below, list what he says about each. How do the three persons of the Trinity interact with each other, according to this letter?

ASSESS THE MAIN IDEA

Based on your study these last three weeks and today's study of Jesus in Colossians, write out the main idea of this book in a single sentence as you understand it today. Make it precise, concise, and memorable. (Consider the following question: What is true about Jesus in Paul's letter to the Colossians?)

SPARK TRANSFORMATION

Allow the Holy Spirit to move you to personal application based on what you've studied today. Ask Him to transform you from the inside out, reshaping the way you think about Jesus, about yourself, and about the world around you. If He leads you, write out a specific application to your life today.

TURN TO GOD IN WORSHIP

What did you learn today about God the Father, Son, and Holy Spirit from your broad reading of Colossians?

"All Creatures of Our God and King" is a hymn written by William H. Draper (1855–1933) based on a poem written by St. Francis of Assisi. Allow these beautiful words lead you in your response in worship:

All creatures of our God and King
Lift up your voice and with us sing,
Alleluia! Alleluia! [. . .]
Let all things their Creator bless,
And worship Him in humbleness,
O praise Him! Alleluia!
Praise, praise the Father, praise the Son,
And praise the Spirit, Three in One!
O praise Him! O praise Him!
Alleluia! Alleluia! Alleluia!

WEEKEND REFLECTION

What did you learn about God this week?

What did you learn about yourself?

In what way is Jesus inviting you to trust that He is enough?

What do you most want to say to God right now?

hidden with Christ

For you died, and your life is now hidden with Christ in God.
COLOSSIANS 3:3

Who is the holiest person you know?

Perhaps a loved one comes to mind. Or a pious person from long ago. Maybe you're thinking of someone who is so much higher on the holiness ladder that you're left feeling "less than."

But here's the thing: if you are in Christ and He is in you, He has declared you holy.

Yes, you.

Yes, with your burdensome secret that you've never told anyone. With your quiet struggles that no one else knows about. With your daily ongoing fight against sin.

In Christ, you are holy.

You are holy because Jesus is the Holy One of God. He is the only One who has never sinned, never tempted anyone else to sin, and who in fact defeated sin in His death and resurrection. He alone is able to clothe us with divine righteousness that we would not have on our own. God declares us holy not because of our moral achievements or because of our sincere obedience, but because of Jesus' holiness.

When God looks at us, He sees the holiness of Jesus covering us like a garment. Before God in heaven, we are already positionally holy even as we grow practically in this holiness day by day, through the power of the Holy Spirit in us.[13]

Sure, you might not "feel" holy, especially after a rough day with the kids or a demanding day at work. But our spiritual confidence lies not in our feelings or our doings, but in the righteousness of Christ alone. He is enough.

As we study the first part of Colossians 3 this week, let's resist the temptation to turn Paul's exhortations into a list of things to do. Instead, let's see it as his invitation to embody here and now what is already true of us as we're hidden with Christ in God.

For you died, AND YOUR LIFE is now hidden with Christ in God.

COLOSSIANS 3:3

WEEK 4 | DAY 1

SNACK ON THE GO

Do you remember the time you asked Jesus Christ to be your personal Lord and Savior?

I was a young child around five or six, in the back seat of my parents' Subaru when I prayed to "ask Jesus into my heart." And while I meant it in all sincerity, I couldn't help but wonder if I had "done it right." So every time I heard a televangelist pray the sinner's prayer, I prayed it too, just in case.

This spiritual doubt is not uncommon among believers, and it causes many to question whether they'll lose their salvation if they do or say the wrong thing. It's in this context that Paul's words to the Colossians provide reassurance:

> For you died, and your life is now hidden with Christ in God.
> **COLOSSIANS 3:3**

Those of us who have accepted Jesus as our personal Lord and Savior have died to the world and to sin and have been raised again into new life with Him. But not only that—our life is "hidden" in God. That means that God holds our eternal salvation securely, hidden as a precious treasure so that no one can steal it or threaten it in any way. If you are a child of God, your eternal security rests in God's powerful and capable hands (see Jesus' words in John 10:29), so rejoice in His salvation and assurance today.

Choose a verse from Colossians 3 to memorize this week, and write it in the space below.

FEAST AT THE TABLE

FOCUS ON GOD

Open your Bible to Psalm 119:68. Write it out as a prayer to the Lord as you begin your study of His Word today.

ENGAGE THE TEXT

Read Colossians 3:1–4 out loud and write it in the space below.

Write out anything that immediately stands out to you.

This passage begins with "Since, then" or "If then," building the practical applications on the doctrinal foundation laid out in the last two chapters. Summarize in two or three sentences the theological truths of Colossians chapters 1–2.

If the first part of Colossians speaks of Jesus' complete adequacy to justify and sanctify believers, then the second part of Colossians fleshes out what that fullness looks like in day-to-day life. But before we jump in, let's be careful to frame these instructions within the context of what we've already learned:

How does the gospel bear fruit (1:5–8 and 1:10–11) in the lives of believers who share in the fullness (2:10) of Jesus Christ?

Is it a self-imposed improvement plan or Spirit-driven transformation?

Colossians 3:1–10 explains what is positionally true of those who believe in Jesus, and then calls upon them to live it out practically. What does this passage say about the believer's position in Christ? The Colossians were becoming practically what they were already were positionally in Jesus Christ. In verses 1–2, Paul calls the Colossians to set both their hearts and minds on "things above." Based on the last two chapters, what "things" is Paul referring to?

What does it mean to set one's heart on things above? And the mind?

How are the two different?

How are they similar?

ASSESS THE MAIN IDEA

In your own words, summarize the meaning of verses 3–4.

What does this say about God?

What does it say about believers?

What does it say about Christ's sufficiency?

SPARK TRANSFORMATION

How does the core belief that Christ is enough and has given you His fullness impact your motivation to live out practically what is already true positionally?

In the space below, list what is already true about you, in Jesus Christ, according to the first two chapters of Colossians.

Look at the list you made last week of ways you try to please God, and make another list of all the ways you try to cover up or compensate for your deficiencies on your own.

What is your fallback to make you feel okay? Food? Makeup? Shopping? Fantasies? Resolutions to try harder? Write it down in the space below.

Ask the Spirit to shine His light in your heart and reveal any idols that capture your attention and affection, then confess them to Him.

TURN TO GOD IN WORSHIP

Because Christ is enough, we no longer need to strive to impress Him with our good behavior (as if we even could) or try to run away through numbing activities. Instead, we can rest in His finished work on the cross and live out the holiness that is already ours in Him through our day-to-day actions.

Today, take time to seek His stillness. Simply be still in His presence. He is enough.

WEEK 4 | DAY 2

SNACK ON THE GO

Throughout history, people have been fighting over the things that make us different, whether nation, location, vocation, education, or gumption. (Okay, I made that last one up, but I couldn't come up with a word ending in -tion that described personality type. But you catch my meaning.)

The truth is that try as we might not to do so, we still tend to divide people by so many distinctions. And that is what makes Jesus Christ's sufficiency that much more beautiful: He transcends barriers and unifies people from various backgrounds in Him.

Read Colossians 3:5–11.

We likely don't think of a division between "barbarian, Scythian," and so on, but what might be the things in your life today that divide you from other women in the body of Christ? List them below.

Paraphrase verse 11 in your own words, using the list you made above. Write it below.

As you close your time in God's Word, ask Him to help you focus on what unites you to your sisters in Christ: the Lord Jesus in you.

FEAST AT THE TABLE

FOCUS ON GOD

Open your Bible to Psalm 119:72. Write it out as a prayer to the Lord as you begin your study of His Word today.

ENGAGE THE TEXT

Read Colossians 3:5–11 out loud and write it in the space below.

Write down anything that stands out to you.

Reread verses 1–11. Make two columns below; on one side, write down what this passage says about believers positionally (i.e., what is already true about them in Jesus Christ) and on the other, write what it says practically (i.e., what believers do as a result).

Read Romans 6:1–14. How do these verses illuminate the truths in today's passage?

How can believers live out the behaviors described in today's passage without falling into the works-based righteousness Paul refutes in chapter 2?

Does Paul advocate an anything-goes approach to Christianity? Explain your answer.

How does salvation by grace lead into sanctification by grace?

What imagery does Paul use in this passage to illustrate the old way of life before Christ and the new way of life in Christ?

One of the refreshing truths of this passage is that our inner self is "being renewed in knowledge in the image of [our] Creator" (v. 10). This verb is present continuous, which means that the action occurs on an ongoing basis, and it is passive voice, which means that the action is done by someone else. In this context, God's Spirit is the One who continually renews believers—in knowledge—into the image of God.

According to verse 10, how do believers live out practically what is already true positionally?

What does this passage reveal about God's character?

ASSESS THE MAIN IDEA

What did this mean to the original audience?

Write out the main idea of this passage in a single sentence. Make it precise, concise, and memorable. (Consider the following question: How does Jesus' impending return compel believers to live today?)

SPARK TRANSFORMATION

With a passage like we read today, it's easy to feel burdened by all the ways we fall short. Indeed, the list isn't even exhaustive, and yet it reveals many hidden sins and strongholds that incapacitate believers today.

As you studied the passage, which ones stood out to you?

Confess to God any way in which you may have allowed these habits to infiltrate your life, and ask the Holy Spirit to help you bear the fruit of His righteousness in your life. Prayerfully consider in what ways you can surrender more and more to the leadership and direction of the Spirit.

TURN TO GOD IN WORSHIP

We can trust His faithfulness to complete the work He has started to do in us. Today, end your time FEASTing on the Word of God by acknowledging your complete dependence and trust in God's faithfulness.

WEEK 4 | DAY 3

SNACK ON THE GO

Turn in your Bible to Colossians 3:12–14 and read the passage out loud.

Paul uses a beautiful clothing metaphor to describe believers' lives in Christ, especially what that looks like in the grace of community.

In your journal or in the margin of this book, outline the shape of a woman. (It's okay if you're not artistic—no one but you is going to see this.) As you reread the passage, sketch an article of clothing for every character trait in the text, like a blouse for compassion, a skirt for kindness, and so on.

You can spend as much or as little time with this as you'd like, but as you draw, I encourage you to direct your heart to the Lord in prayer. Ask Him to make these true in your life, through the power of His Holy Spirit in you. And over the next few days, as you get dressed in the morning, ask the Lord to clothe you spiritually as well.

FEAST AT THE TABLE

FOCUS ON GOD

Open your Bible to Psalm 119:73. Write it out as a prayer to the Lord as you begin your study of His Word today.

ENGAGE THE TEXT

Read Colossians 3:12–17 out loud and write it in the space below.

Write down any observations that stand out to you.

"Therefore." What is it there for? Review the preceding passage to familiarize your-self with Paul's previous statements, and write a sentence summarizing his main points in verses 3–11.

What does it mean that believers are "God's chosen people"? What does the term "chosen" imply?

This passage is such a beautiful description of how to live in harmony with community. We'll look more closely at each of the imperatives, but before Paul tells the Colossians what to do, he reminds them that they're "holy and dearly loved."

What do each of those terms mean? (Consider looking them up in a Bible dictionary.)

Why are they important to keep in mind as we head into this passage?

Colossians 3:5–14 uses a clothing metaphor to describe the transition between believers' former way of life and their new life in Christ. List the behavior that Paul admonishes his listeners to demonstrate.

How do each of these practical behaviors in today's passage build on the positional truths explored yesterday?

What does the imagery of clothing communicate?

How are believers to love?

How are believers to forgive?

ASSESS THE MAIN IDEA

What did this text mean to the original audience?

SPARK TRANSFORMATION

As you studied today's passage, is there a particular word or phrase that stood out to you?

Is there someone in your life that you need to forgive? Someone you need God's supernatural forbearance to love like He loves? To treat with more compassion? Or gentleness?

Have you been striving to be more "Christlike" in your own power? The Lord wants you to rest in Him in the assurance that you are chosen and dearly loved. In the space below, write out a prayer responding to the new way of life that Jesus is calling you to.

TURN TO GOD IN WORSHIP

As you end your study in God's Word today, remember that Jesus does not call us to anything He has not already experienced Himself when He walked this earth as fully God and fully man. He was and is chosen by God, holy, and dearly loved.

Reread today's passage, pausing at each descriptor to praise Jesus for the ways He lived out the example of each of these characteristics. If you've stored up Bible stories about Jesus in your heart, recall those scenes from the gospels to mind that illustrate Jesus' compassion, humility, and so on. Spend time in the quietness of your soul watching Jesus interact with the crowds that pushed in on Him, with the self-righteous Pharisees, and with the desperate sinners who knew they needed Him. Listen to how He responds to them. And worship the One who perfectly exemplifies a life of love.

WEEK 4 | DAY 4

SNACK ON THE GO

Gratitude.

It's one of the first social skills we teach children to practice, the art of saying "Thank you." And for good reason—we want children to acknowledge favors, whether it's a birthday gift or a well-meaning gesundheit.

But sometimes, in the busyness of life, it's easy for us to forget these basic manners in our relationship with God. We get so busy that we fail to recognize the daily graces God places in our lives and fail to thank Him for them.

> Let the peace of Christ rule in your hearts, since as members of one body you were called to peace. And be thankful. COLOSSIANS 3:15

"Be thankful," Paul instructs the Colossians, his children in the faith. And the same applies to us today.

I invite you to a simple gratitude challenge: over the next two weeks, take time every day to write down three things you're thankful for. You can write these in your journal, or you can invite your family to join you by posting a list on the fridge everyone can contribute to.

But the important thing is this: as you recognize a gift, don't just write it down— pause to say, "Thank You, Lord. You didn't have to do that, but You did." And allow your thankfulness to lead you in worship.

FEAST AT THE TABLE

FOCUS ON GOD

Open your Bible to Psalm 119:76–77. Write it out as a prayer to the Lord as you begin your study of His Word today.

ENGAGE THE TEXT

Read Colossians 3:15 out loud, then write it in the space below.

Write down any observations that immediately stand out to you.

Look up the meaning of the Greek word translated "peace" in this verse and write out the definition below.

Does the word "rule" stand out to you as it did to me? What images come to mind when you think of something that rules?

Now look up the meaning of the Greek word translated "rule," and write it out below. What does it mean for Christ's peace to "rule" in one's heart?

Although this verse applies to believers individually, Paul was writing to a local church corporately. What words in this verse indicate he may have in mind a plural meaning rather than a singular?

This isn't the first time in his letters Paul's used the imagery of a body to illustrate the unity of the church. Turn to 1 Corinthians 12:12–31. After reading the passage, write a brief summary of what Paul says there about the body.

How does the passage in 1 Corinthians relate to peace? What about love?

Continue reading into 1 Corinthians 13. What do these passages teach about unity in the body of Christ?

There's a short phrase at the end of Colossians 3:15, looking almost like an after-thought. But it packs a punch. What does thankfulness have to do with peace, love, forgiveness, and everything else Paul discusses in the previous verses?

What else stands out to you?

ASSESS THE MAIN IDEA

Write out the main idea of this passage in a single sentence. Make it precise, concise, and memorable. (Consider the following question: What does it look like for Christ's peace to rule in a local body of believers?)

SPARK TRANSFORMATION

As you consider your heart, is it ruled by Jesus Christ's peace or by something else? Tyranny of the urgent? Regrets of the past? Bitterness or resentment? Fear of missing out? Something else?

What would it look like for your heart to be ruled?

Ruled by Jesus?

Ruled by His peace?

How does a peaceful heart affect your interaction with your sisters and brothers in Christ?

And what role does thankfulness play in all this?

Consider starting a new habit of practicing thankfulness. Allow yourself to take time each day to be still and reflect on the previous day, taking time to recognize Jesus' presence in the little details as well as the big. Perhaps even write these gifts down in a notebook or journal you keep just for this purpose.

TURN TO GOD IN WORSHIP

"It Is Well with My Soul" was written by Horatio Spafford (1828–1888). Allow the following lyrics from this beloved hymn to lead your time of worship:

> When peace, like a river, attendeth my way,
> When sorrows like sea billows roll;
> Whatever my lot, Thou hast taught me to say,
> It is well, it is well with my soul.
> It is well with my soul,
> It is well, it is well with my soul.

WEEK 4 | DAY 5

SNACK ON THE GO

Can you eat a cookie for the glory of God?

It sounds like a silly question, but it's a practical application of what Paul means when he says, "Whatever you do, whether in word or deed, do it all in the name of the Lord Jesus, giving thanks to God the Father through Him" (Col. 3:17).

In a related passage in 1 Corinthians 10:31, Paul specifically states "whether you eat or drink," you should do it "for the glory of God." So what does it mean to do something in Jesus' name and for His glory?

It means that our daily actions should reflect the heavenly realities that supersede our present circumstances. In other words, the way we fix our kids' breakfast, the way we present in a board meeting, the way we volunteer at church, or even the way we eat a cookie should flow out of the sufficiency of Jesus Christ and the fullness we have received from Him.

Because Jesus Christ is above all and in all, His preeminence influences every single choice we make. So how can you point to the surpassing sweetness in your choices today?

FEAST AT THE TABLE
FOCUS ON GOD

Open your Bible to Psalm 119:89–90. Write it out as a prayer to the Lord as you begin your study of His Word today.

ENGAGE THE TEXT

Read Colossians 3:16–17 out loud, then write it in the space below.

Write down any observations that immediately stand out to you.

What does the word "dwell" mean? How is this imagery different from a visit?

In what ways did Paul expect the Colossians to practice the indwelling of God's Word?

Look up the following passages on each topic, and write down what stands out to you as you read:

- Psalms: Luke 20:42, 24:44; Acts 1:20, 13:33

- Hymns: Mark 14:26; Acts 16:25; Hebrews 2:12

- Spiritual songs: Ephesians 5:19; Revelation 5:9, 14:3, 15:3

How are all these similar?

How are they different?

For examples of Christian hymns that would have been sung during the writing of this letter, look up the following:

- Colossians 1:15–20

- Ephesians 5:14

• Philippians 2:6–11

• 1 Timothy 3:16

What do these passages have in common?

How do they exemplify the word of Christ dwelling richly?

ASSESS THE MAIN IDEA

What did today's passage mean to the original audience?

SPARK TRANSFORMATION

If you're looking for a passage to memorize, Colossians 3:12–17 is a great one to start with. Sure, it's a chunk, but it's just six verses in all. If you took it slowly, a verse at a time, could you memorize one per month? Then you'll have this passage in half a year, which might not sound impressive, but it's probably still more than most of us are memorizing on a regular basis. And the Word of God never returns to Him void. You never know when the Holy Spirit will bring these words to mind when you most need them. Alternately, write out one or more verses on a card and place it somewhere prominent where you'll see it every day and be reminded of its truths.

One of the easiest ways to memorize large chunks of information is through song. This is why many children learn their ABCs to the tune of "Twinkle Twinkle Little Star," which also incidentally is the same tune as "Baa Baa Black Sheep" and many other nursery rhymes. (Have you ever noticed that? Weird, huh?) Yet as adults, we sometimes shun silly rhymes and tunes as beneath us. But what if we adapted this method and began using music to memorize Scripture and doctrine?

If you feel like you just can't memorize Bible verses, consider this challenge: find an album that's simply Scripture set to music. (There are plenty of children's CDs to choose from, but I've also found music geared for adults as well.) It doesn't matter which one you pick—just pick one album with several tracks. Then for the next seven days, listen exclusively to this Scripture-song album. No radio. No iTunes. No throwback 70s. Just Scripture songs, at least once a day. At the end of the seven days, you'll find that not only have you memorized several verses, but you'll probably find that they're coming to mind throughout your day, even when you're not playing the album. This is the power of music, and it is exactly how God wired our brains to help us remember essential truths. Are you up for the challenge?

TURN TO GOD IN WORSHIP

Throughout this study we've been using the words of Psalm 119 to prepare our heart to focus on God as we begin to study His Word. When I first started using this FEAST method, I sometimes felt like I didn't have the words to pray, but eventually I realized that God had already given me 176 daily prayers for beginning my Bible study in the verses of this, the longest psalm of the Bible. What a remarkable provision He's given us! As you end your time FEASTing on God's Word, turn back to Psalm 119 and allow His Words to guide you in worship and praise.

WEEKEND REFLECTION

What did you learn about God this week?

What did you learn about yourself?

In what way is Jesus inviting you to trust that He is enough?

What do you most want to say to God right now?

loving like Christ

Whatever you do, work at it with all your heart, as working for the Lord, not for human masters. **COLOSSIANS 3:23**

What's the most demanding relationship in your life right now?

You know, that person who gets on your last nerve but you feel like you really should be nicer to. The one who can affect your whole day with just a few syllables. The one you *just can't stand.*

That person.

What would it look like to love that person like Jesus?

I know, I know. You're going to jump in and protest, "But you don't know what she . . ." "You have no idea how he . . ." "If only you were there when . . ."

Please listen, dear one. I get it. Really. There are people in my life and yours who have hurt us beyond anything imaginable. There are legitimate times when boundaries are necessary to protect us or our loved ones' physical, mental, and emotional well-being. There are relationships that have shattered to a degree that no amount of greeting cards or birthday gifts will ever restore.

And yet, God calls us to love them.

Love them not because they're loveable, but love them because He loves us . . . and He also loves them.

If we read our next passage in Colossians out of context, we could easily feel stifled by the rules Paul lays out for relationships. We can bristle when we hear words like "submit" and "obey" and "serve."

But as we read Colossians 3:18–4:4 in its proper context, we'll realize that what Paul lays out truly is impossible . . . without Jesus. On our own, we cannot love our spouses, children, parents, supervisors, subordinates, church family, and community the way God calls us to. Absolutely not possible.

And yet, when we read these principles within the larger context of who Jesus is (chapters 1–2) and who we are in Him (chapter 3:1–17), we understand that Christ's love moves us to freely seek each other's highest interest in all relationships. Because of how generously we have been loved, we can allow Christ's love to flow through us.

This isn't about fabricating warm and fuzzy feelings. It's not about squaring our shoulders and trying harder. It's about allowing the fullness of Jesus to fill us in our most broken relationships, and inviting Him to love others in and through us. Because on our own, we cannot love the unlovable. But through Him we can. Because He is enough.

Whatever you do, work at it with all your heart, as working for the LORD, not for human masters.

COLOSSIANS 3:23

WEEK 5 | DAY 1

SNACK ON THE GO

Open your Bible to Colossians 3:18–19. As you read these verses, observe your own reaction to them, and ask the Holy Spirit to help you set aside preconceptions and misunderstandings of the text. Sit with this passage for a few moments, and allow your heart to grow still.

These instructions for marriage are rooted in the relationship between Jesus and His bride. Flip over to Ephesians 5:22–33 and observe: How does Jesus love His bride, the church, and how is He gentle with her?

How is the church to submit to Jesus and trust His leadership?

What is one thing you've learned about Jesus in today's reading? How can you respond to Him today?

FEAST AT THE TABLE

FOCUS ON GOD

Open your Bible to Psalm 119:97. Write it out as a prayer to the Lord as you begin your study of His Word today.

ENGAGE THE TEXT

Read Colossians 3:18–19 out loud and write it in the space below.

Write down your observations.

Read Ephesians 5:22–33 for a parallel passage that provides more details, and add any additional observations or questions that come up.

The passages we'll read this week have been abused and misused for evil purposes throughout history, but as we study Scripture, we humbly ask God's Spirit to help us set our preconceptions aside and seek His heart. Married or single, youth or adult, male or female, each of Paul's recipients would have been included in these rules for family relationships.

How does this passage build on the previous texts we've studied?

Why is it important to keep this foundational context in mind before diving into application?

According to the Ephesians passage, what relationship should Christ-centered marriages model?

How are wives to relate to their husbands?

What does the phrase "as is fitting in the Lord" add to the meaning of this instruction?

How are husbands to relate to their wives?

In what way does Ephesians 5:21, which immediately precedes the parallel passage in Ephesians, inform our interpretation of Paul's instruction for wives?

How are husbands called to mutual submission, in the instruction given to them?

How does Colossians 3:12–17 also influence the meaning of these family rules?

How does the reality of Christ's presence, sufficiency, and supremacy affect marital relationships?

What else stands out to you in this passage?

ASSESS THE MAIN IDEA

Wives are called to submit to their husbands, and this word, "submit," carries a lot of baggage for twenty-first-century readers, but it would have meant something entirely different for Paul's first-century readers. Look up the nonmilitary use of the word here in a Bible dictionary, and write down what this exhortation would have meant for Paul's first-century audience.

Notice that wives are called to submit; the word "obey" does not appear in Scripture in respect to wives (as it does for children and slaves). How is submission different from obedience?

What would this passage have meant to the original audience? Consider answering the question: How does the reality that Jesus is enough affect one's marriage relationship?

SPARK TRANSFORMATION

How does today's main idea apply to your life directly?

What is one way you can immediately put this into practice?

TURN TO GOD IN WORSHIP

Those who are filled with God's Holy Spirit love each other in radically different ways from the ways the world loves.

How does the metaphor of marriage speak of the love God has for us and the way we are called to respond to His love?

What does that say about God?

Today, recite His goodness, speaking out loud the beautiful attributes you see in the reading and praising Him for being such a loving God.

WEEK 5 | DAY 2

SNACK ON THE GO

My mother-in-law loves to tell the story of how my husband came home from Sunday school one day and, ornery as he was, informed his parents that he had learned a Bible verse. Delighted, they asked that he recite it for them, and he promptly said, "Parents, obey your children in everything, for this pleases the Lord."

I guess you could say our children take after him, precocious as they are. But as a parent now myself, I marvel at the love and humility expressed in Scripture whenever it refers to the ways we are to relate to each other. While parents are not called to obey their children (much to our kids' dismay), they are called to cherish and even honor them in a different way:

> Fathers, do not embitter your children, or they will become discouraged. COLOSSIANS 3:21

Throughout Scripture, whenever someone is given authority over another, they are charged to nurture, care for, protect, and seek the best for those who look up to them. This relationship rooted in love is modeled after our own Father's heart for us. His love for us knows no limits, and His patience is beyond understanding. In the same way, whether we're parents or children, wives or husbands, employee or employer, we are to show sacrificial love and seek others' highest good before our own.

How can you honor your parents today?

If you have children at home, how can you show them love today?

FEAST AT THE TABLE

FOCUS ON GOD

Open your Bible to Psalm 119:103. Write it out as a prayer to the Lord as you begin your study of His Word today.

ENGAGE THE TEXT

Read Colossians 3:20–21 out loud and write it in the space below.

Write down any immediate observations that come to mind.

What is the main reason children should obey their parents, according to verse 20?

How are fathers to relate to their children? What reasoning does Paul provide in verse 21?

What's the opposite of embittering (or exasperating) someone? How is this illustrated in the instructions Paul provides in Colossians 3:8–17?

Read Ephesians 6:1–4 for a parallel passage that provides more details, and add any additional observations or questions that come up.

As you consider verses 18–21, what does Paul's care for every member of the household reveal about the value of all people, whoever they are?

How does the reality of Christ's presence, sufficiency, and supremacy affect parent-child relationships?

What else stands out to you in today's passage?

ASSESS THE MAIN IDEA

Before you interpret this passage, consider the following notes on the text:

> The Greek word for *fathers (pateres)* can sometimes refer to both parents, as in Hebrews 11:23. . . . The standard Greek lexicon of the New Testament suggests that this is what the word means here in Colossians. . . . However, the primary referent is probably the father, since this fits the culture of that time, in which the man was the head of the household and would have had primary responsibility for issuing orders to children. The Romans called this power *patria potestas,* "the power of the father," and it was a basic assumption about the way the household in the Hellenistic world should function. . . . And certainly, a reference to mothers as well as fathers is justified from the standpoint of cultural translation.[14]

What did this mean to the original audience?

In what ways does Jesus' sufficiency affect parent-child relationships?

SPARK TRANSFORMATION

How does this passage apply to your life?

How might you show honor toward your parents and love toward your children (if applicable) this week?

TURN TO GOD IN WORSHIP

How does the heavenly Father's love for His children model the type of parenting that Paul says should take place in believers' families?

In what ways has God shown you this kind of love in your own life?

Take a few moments today to respond to God in worship. What do you most want to say to Him?

WEEK 5 | DAY 3

SNACK ON THE GO

Whether we're sweeping Cheerios off a sticky floor or swaying a stoic-like audience with our presentation, there will always be parts of our work in life that are less than enjoyable. In the space below, list two or three responsibilities that you'd happily hand off to someone else.

While we may not have the luxury to outsource these chores, we do have a choice in how we do them. Paul speaks to this very situation when he instructs the Colossian church. In the space below, write out Colossians 3:23–24:

It is the Lord Christ you are serving. Even when cleaning toilets? Even when entering mind-numbing data? Even when driving zigzags around town to drop off and pick up everyone from their activities? Yes. Even then. It's for the Lord Christ.

How energetically would we match and fold socks if we knew that Jesus would wear them?

Yes, it's a laughable thought, but really, Jesus says that when we serve even one of the most insignificant persons in the room, we're serving Him.

Take one of the tasks you've listed above, and ask God to give you a fresh perspective and to help you serve Him in doing it. May He be pleased with your work.

FEAST AT THE TABLE

FOCUS ON GOD

Open your Bible to Psalm 119:105. Write it out as a prayer to the Lord as you begin your study of His Word today.

ENGAGE THE TEXT

Read Colossians 3:22–4:1 out loud and write it in the space below.

Engage the passage by writing down observations. What does the passage say? Try answering the five Ws: who, what, when, where, why? And perhaps also how?

Read Ephesians 6:5–9 for a parallel passage that provides more details, and add any additional observations or questions that come up.

What other passages relate to today's text? Look up those cross-references, and write down additional observations. (See the sidebar in Week Two, Day One for tips on checking cross-references.)

How are slaves to serve their masters? List out each instruction in the space below, and write out observations on each.

How does Paul instruct masters to treat their slaves? How would this instruction have been countercultural?

What motivation does Paul give for his instructions?

What Christian principles does Paul call both slaves and masters to demonstrate in their relationships with each other?

How does the preceding passage in Colossians 3:12–17 apply to this relationship of slave/master?

How does the reality of Christ's presence and sufficiency affect how slaves were to serve their masters? What about how masters were to treat their slaves?

What else stands out to you in this passage?

ASSESS THE MAIN IDEA

To some readers, Paul's words to slaves and masters may prove problematic. To help us understand the first-century household relationship of slave-master, read the following commentary on this text:

> At first sight, Paul's command that slaves obey their masters seems simply to endorse the status quo. But we need to see that what he writes here also subtly undermines it. First, it is significant that Paul chooses to address slaves at all, implying not only that they are assembled with the other Christians of the Colossian church to hear the letter being read but that they are responsible people who need to choose a certain kind of behavior. Second, Paul clearly relativizes the status of the slave's master by repeatedly reminding both slave (vv. 22, 23, 24) and master (4:1) of the ultimate "master" to whom both are responsible: the Lord Jesus Christ. Third, Paul never hints that he endorses the institution of slavery. He tells slaves and masters how they are to conduct themselves within the institution, but it is a bad misreading of Paul to read into his teaching approval of the institution itself.[15]

Write out the main idea of this passage in a single sentence. Make it precise, concise, and memorable. (Consider the following question: How does the sufficiency of Jesus affect how first-century workers were to relate to their employers and vice versa?)

SPARK TRANSFORMATION

Ask the Holy Spirit to spark transformation in your life through practical application. Ask Him, "How does this apply to me?" and write down your answer in the space below.

TURN TO GOD IN WORSHIP

Turn your mind and heart toward God in worship. What do you most want to say to God?

WEEK 5 | DAY 4

SNACK ON THE GO

Open your Bible and read Colossians 4:2, first silently and then aloud. Then write it in the space below.

What's one thing that stands out to you in this verse?

How does this apply to your life today?

Come up with hand motions for "devote," "prayer," "watchful," and "thankful." Now read the verse aloud three more times, using the hand motions you've assigned.

Close your Bible, and try reciting the verse, using only your hand motions.

Congratulations! You've memorized your verse for the week! Throughout the day, recite your verse, taking a moment afterward to turn to the Lord in prayer.

FEAST AT THE TABLE

FOCUS ON GOD

Open your Bible to Psalm 119:108. Write it out as a prayer to the Lord as you begin your study of His Word today.

ENGAGE THE TEXT

Today we'll be studying a single verse, but reading the context to better understand it. Read Colossians 4:2–6 out loud, and write verse 2 below.

Write down any observations that immediately come to mind.

Now let's focus on verse 2. How does prayer lay the foundation for the other instructions in this passage?

What is prayer?

According to this passage, who should be praying?

What do you think it means to be devoted to prayer?

Read Luke 18:1–8 and summarize what Jesus says about devoted prayer in a single sentence. How does it compare to your response to the previous question?

Paul describes the Colossians' prayer lives with two words: *watchful* and *thankful*. What does it mean to be watchful in prayer?

What about being thankful? How does this focus on prayer find its foundation in the sufficiency of Jesus Christ, as described in chapters 1–2?

If believers are to be devoted to conversation with God, what does that tell us about God?

Read Hebrews 4:14–16. What does this passage teach us about God's posture toward our prayers?

What else stands out to you in Colossians 4:2–6?

ASSESS THE MAIN IDEA

As you look at your observations above, take a step back to interpret the meaning of all you've written. Write out the main idea in a single sentence. Make it precise, concise, and memorable. (Consider answering the following question: How does the sufficiency of Jesus affect how believers should approach prayer?)

SPARK TRANSFORMATION

On a scale of one to ten, how important would you rate prayer in your life?

If a stranger followed you around for a week, would they agree with your assessment, based on an objective look at your actions?

Is there something in your life that needs to change so that your actions about prayer better match your beliefs? What would it look like for you to be devoted in prayer right in this season of your life?

TURN TO GOD IN WORSHIP

Take a moment today to thank Jesus for being our High Priest who intercedes for us and welcomes us to His throne of grace with confidence. Write your prayer below.

WEEK 5 | DAY 5

SNACK ON THE GO

People in ministry often come against much opposition, both spiritually and physically.

In today's passage, Paul asks the Colossians to pray for him and his fellow coworkers in ministry. Open your Bible to Colossians 4:3–4 and read the passage aloud.

As you reflect on your own life, who do you turn to for spiritual nourishment? List below the names of your pastor, women's ministry leader, Sunday school teacher, and any Christian authors or teachers you regularly listen to or read.

Using today's passage as a guide, write out a prayer for these men and women and their ministries in the space below.

As you finish, consider praying for these ministers on a regular basis, perhaps on Sunday morning as you get ready for church or on any other day you choose. Set a calendar notification to remind you to pray for those who serve you.

FEAST AT THE TABLE

My goal with this study is not just to lead you deeper in your relationship with Jesus, but also to help you become confident in your own Bible study skills. So today we'll be doing a solo study, where you take the techniques we've been using the past few weeks and apply them on your own as you study Scripture. You may use the FEAST method if you'd like, but feel free to follow the Holy Spirit's lead.

FOCUS ON GOD

Ask the Lord, "What do You want me to learn?" Consider using a passage of Scripture as during previous days' studies to center your heart and mind on God.

ENGAGE THE TEXT

Read Colossians 4:3–4 and write it in the space below.

Ask yourself, "What does the text say?" Consider asking the five journalistic questions: who, what, when, where, why?

ASSESS THE MAIN IDEA

Answer the question, "What did this mean to the original audience?"

SPARK TRANSFORMATION

Ask the Holy Spirit to transform you, answering the question, "How does this apply to my life?"

TURN TO GOD IN WORSHIP

Ask yourself, "How do I want to respond to God?"

WEEKEND REFLECTION

What did you learn about God this week?

What did you learn about yourself?

In what way is Jesus inviting you to trust that He is enough?

What do you most want to say to God right now?

ministering with Christ

Be wise in the way you act toward outsiders; make the most of every opportunity. COLOSSIANS 4:5

What would it be like to serve under Jesus' rule?

I mean, imagine Him ruling over the world, seated in His temple in Jerusalem, and He's given you a special assignment to carry out on His behalf. What would that assignment be?

According to the many prophecies in Revelation, Isaiah, and throughout Scripture, that's the reality that we'll be living in soon. One day, Jesus will return as the King of kings, He will establish His kingdom here on earth, and we will rule with Him and serve under Him. But we don't have to wait until then to begin living on His mission—we can begin here and now.

In fact, even though Paul doesn't reference Jesus' return in his letter to the Colossians as he does in his other letters, he introduces this theme of ministering with Christ early in chapter 1 and returns to it here in chapter 4. The gospel is bearing fruit and growing all over the world, and we are invited to participate in this work through our devoted prayers, grace-filled conversations, and hands-on involvement in the work of the gospel.

As we'll see this week, you don't have to be a pastor, an evangelist, or a missionary to participate with Jesus in His mission here on earth. God has already placed you right where He wants you, and in Christ He's given you everything you need to advance the gospel right where you are. It's Jesus that we're sharing with those around us.

"For in Christ all the fullness of the Deity lives in bodily form, and in Christ you have been brought to fullness. He is the head over every power and authority" (Col. 2:9–10). We don't need to try hard to convince others He's worth it. We don't have to worry about what we'll say or how we'll bring up these matters in conversation. We need only to invite people to come to Him. His Spirit will do the rest. Because Jesus is enough.

Be wise in the way you act toward outsiders; make the most of every opportunity.

COLOSSIANS 4:5

WEEK 6 | DAY 1

SNACK ON THE GO

There's much wisdom to be found in children's cartoons. One line in particular has stuck with me throughout my childhood and adult life because it comes from the classic film *Bambi* when Thumper advised: "If you can't say something nice, don't say nothing at all."

How many inflaming internet discussions and heart-wrenching in-person confrontations would be dissolved if only we heeded that little bunny's advice? (He had a wise mama.) Those words may have been inspired by Paul's similar instruction to the first-century church in Colossae:

> Let your conversation be always full of grace, seasoned with salt, so that you may know how to answer everyone. COLOSSIANS 4:6

Paul may have taken his cue from Jesus' Sermon on the Mount, when He said that those who follow Him are the salt of the earth (Matt. 5:13). Salt was known to the ancient world as a preservative, slowing down rot and decay, and a taste enhancer. As such, our words should lessen the decay surrounding us and enhance the wholesome beauty all around us.

Today, ask the Holy Spirit to fill you with His Word so that your every word would encourage and bring grace to the listener.

FEAST AT THE TABLE

FOCUS ON GOD

Open your Bible to Psalm 119:114. Write it out as a prayer to the Lord as you begin your study of His Word today.

ENGAGE THE TEXT

Read Colossians 4:5–6 out loud and write it in the space below.

In this context, what does it mean to "make the most of every opportunity"?

What does it mean to "be wise" in interactions with others?

How does 1 Peter 3:15–16 clarify the manner in which believers are to be wise toward "outsiders"?

What does verse 6 say about the tone of believers when speaking with unbelievers?

Based on everything Paul has said in this letter so far, why does he stress the importance of conduct toward unbelievers?

How does prayer (vv. 2–4) prepare believers to proclaim the gospel?

How does a life saturated in prayer lead to living out verses 5 and 6?

As we consider this passage and also 1 Peter 3:15–16, what is our part as believers in sharing the gospel?

Who is ultimately responsible for the results?

What does this passage say about believers' conversations?

What does "seasoned with salt" mean?[16] Look up Mark 9:50 for Jesus' words on this, and write your observations below.

ASSESS THE MAIN IDEA

Write out the main idea of this passage in a single sentence. Make it precise, concise, and memorable. (Consider the following question: How does the sufficiency of Jesus Christ influence believers' interactions with unbelievers?)

SPARK TRANSFORMATION

As you studied today's passage, is there someone in particular who comes to mind? Someone you can pray for a door to be opened, and the gospel proclaimed to that person?

Ask the Holy Spirit to help you respond in a way that is SMART: specific, measurable, attainable, realistic, and time-bound.

TURN TO GOD IN WORSHIP

Prayer and evangelism are two disciplines that oftentimes elicit feelings of guilt in Christians today. What is your reaction to today's passage?

Instead of allowing guilt to overwhelm you, read Hebrews 4:14–16, then worship Jesus for His gracious response to our deep need for Him, and spend a few moments being still before Him, knowing He understands exactly where you are and what your struggles are. If there are areas of unconfessed sin, acknowledge them to Him and receive His forgiveness and restoration, and celebrate His closeness in your place of need. Then ask for and receive His mercy and grace to help you live a life worthy of Him, always prepared to give an answer for the hope within you (1 Peter 3:15) not because you are able but because He is enough.

WEEK 6 | DAY 2

SNACK ON THE GO

Open your Bible and read Colossians 4:7–9.

Okay, you might not understand who these people are or what these instructions mean, but that's okay. Today, we're just going to take a look at how they're described. Read these verses again, paying attention to the words Paul uses to describe Tychicus and Onesimus. List those words below.

Pick one adjective you wrote above, and think about what it means. You might even want to look it up in a dictionary. What does it look like in day-to-day life? In ministry?

As you reflect on your own life, do you think your pastor or women's ministry leader would say this same word is true of you?

In the space below, try it out. Write your name, and then the description you chose from the list.

_____ is _____.

             [NAME]   [DESCRIPTION]

What would it look like for you to live into that reality? Today, make it your prayer, asking the Lord to make it true of your life.

FEAST AT THE TABLE

FOCUS ON GOD

Open your Bible to Psalm 119:124. Write it out as a prayer to the Lord as you begin your study of His Word today.

ENGAGE THE TEXT

Read Colossians 4:7–9 out loud and write it in the space below.

Write down anything that stands out to you.

How is Tychicus described in verse 7? What do each of the three phrases mean?

Look up each of the following cross-references about Tychicus, and list what you learn about this person:

EPHESIANS 6:21–22

2 TIMOTHY 4:12

TITUS 3:12

Who was Tychicus? What did he do? What was his role in the first-century church?

In light of Paul's instruction in Colossians 3:22–25, what is the significance of Paul using servant/Lord terminology in reference to Tychicus?

Colossians 4:9 refers to Onesimus. How is he described?

How is this similar to and different from Tychicus's description?

Before we move on, what do you already know about Onesimus?

Now turn in your Bible to the book of Philemon, and quickly skim this letter Paul wrote at the same time he wrote Colossians and delivered by the same men. What is Paul's main point in this brief letter?

What does this letter reveal about Onesimus and how had he wronged Philemon?

Under Roman law, Onesimus's actions were punishable by death, but Paul appeals to Philemon to forgive and to receive him as a brother. How does this dynamic between Onesimus and Philemon (and Paul's appeal to Philemon) illustrate Paul's teaching in Colossians 3:22–4:1?

Which of the relational dynamics found in 3:22–4:1 also surface in this relationship between Onesimus and Philemon?

What would their relationship look like if they both applied this teaching to their lives?

How does Paul describe himself in Philemon (vv. 1, 9, and 23)?

How does this contrast with how he describes himself in Colossians (1:1)?

Why would Paul use this different language, in light of his appeal to Philemon?

How does Paul's description of Onesimus in Colossians compare to his description of him in Philemon verse 16?

ASSESS THE MEANING

Write out the main idea of Colossians 4:7–9 in a single sentence. Make it precise, concise, and memorable. (Consider the following question: What does the study of these two men, Tychicus and Onesimus, reveal about Christian relationships and service, in light of the sufficiency and supremacy of Jesus explained in chapters 1–2?)

SPARK TRANSFORMATION

The relational dynamic between Onesimus and Philemon is clearly filled with tension, demonstrated by Paul's initiative to personally appeal to Philemon, a unique missive in the New Testament epistles. But the fact that this relationship and these letters are preserved for us in Scripture give us hope that in our own less-than-perfect relationships, we can move toward harmony and reconciliation.

What's a relationship in your life right now that feels strained?

What might it look like to "bear with each other and forgive one another if any of you has a grievance against someone" (3:13) in this relationship?

Interestingly enough, we don't get to see the end of this relational drama. We don't know how Philemon reacted when he received Paul's letter, or what he did when he saw Onesimus upon his return. But that's not the point. Onesimus returned to Philemon, in humble submission to Paul's instruction in 3:22–25, and in full confidence of who he was in Christ and with Christ (see chapters 1–2). Philemon's response was entirely up to him, as is our response today.

What is the Holy Spirit calling you to do in this relationship He brought to mind?

In the space below, write a short prayer expressing to God humble submission and love, confident that Christ is enough regardless of the other person's response to you.

TURN TO GOD IN WORSHIP

As you end your time feasting on Scripture, pause to acknowledge the lordship of Jesus Christ over all your activities and all your relationships. Surrender all you are to all He is. You might want to use Philippians 2:1–11 to guide your response in worship.

WEEK 6 | DAY 3

SNACK ON THE GO

In the spectrum of Christian activities, prayer seems to have a reputation of being a passive activity, while evangelism and activism seem to be more on the active side. It's easy to look at those Christians who are involved in "flashy" Christian service, such as those on the stage or in "professional" Christian ministry, and feel like our own contribution of devoted prayer in comparison is paltry.

But Scripture presents a different view of prayer. Write Colossians 4:12 in the space below:

This word "wrestling" is anything but passive. It depicts a battle in the spiritual realm, pointing to the truth that "our struggle is not against flesh and blood, but against the rulers, against the authorities, against the powers of this dark world and against the spiritual forces of evil in the heavenly realms" (Eph. 6:12). That's intense.

Epaphras, the man Paul describes here, had brought the gospel to the Colossians (see 1:7) and he was probably the one teaching and leading the church there. But much of his work was done behind the scenes, in his secret prayer closet. This man understood that his outward-facing spiritual activities were only as powerful as his inner life of prayer, and he was devoted to wrestling for those he loved in his prayers.

When you think of your own prayer life, where would you place it on the passive to active scale?

1 _____ 10

(PASSIVE)   (ACTIVE)

What would it look like to wrestle in prayer on behalf of those you love?

Write a prayer to Jesus, asking Him to fill you with the desire and urgency to wrestle in prayer for those He has placed in your life. Ask Him to show you what that looks like, and to train you in wrestling prayer.

FEAST AT THE TABLE

FOCUS ON GOD

Open your Bible to Psalm 119:127–128. Write it out as a prayer to the Lord as you begin your study of His Word today.

ENGAGE THE TEXT

Read Colossians 4:10–14 out loud and write it in the space below.

Write down any immediate observations that come to mind.

Paul typically closes his epistles with greetings and a list of names that makes most of us want to skim over the verses to get to the end. But today we're going to dig in and uncover the beauty of these kinds of passages. Make a list of all the names Paul mentions in this passage, and next to each include any details provided about them.

What does this list signify about the way Paul did ministry?

Read 1 Corinthians 12:12–30 and summarize how these final greetings in Colossians exemplify the central truth of the Corinthian passage.

Pick a name in the list and look up the cross-references, writing down additional details as you find them, just as we did with Tychicus and Onesimus in yesterday's study of verses 7–9.

Pull out a Bible map (or look one up online) and plot the locations mentioned in this section, including Rome, the city where Paul was imprisoned when he wrote this letter. How does this closing passage demonstrate the truth of Paul's opening words in Colossians 1:3–8?

Epaphras, who likely planted the church in Colossae, is a remarkable example of a leader who toiled for his church not just in public but in private too. In 4:12 we're given a beautiful picture of active, involved, intense prayer, or as Paul puts it, "wrestling in prayer" for his congregation. What kind of a picture does this phrase of "wrestling in prayer" paint? What might that look like in daily life?

This closing greeting seems almost an appendix to the rest of the letter, but it's still relevant and related. How does Paul's inclusion of his coworkers for the gospel relate to the previous three chapters in Colossians?

ASSESS THE MAIN IDEA

Write out the main idea of this passage in a single sentence. Make it precise, concise, and memorable.

SPARK TRANSFORMATION

Why is it important to surround ourselves with others who are devoted to Christ and to His work?

In your own life, do you have godly women who encourage you to go deeper in your relationship with Jesus and to serve others? If so, list their names below and thank God for their involvement in your life. If not, write a prayer asking Him to give you godly friends and mentors.

TURN TO GOD IN WORSHIP

What does this passage reveal about God? Spend some time responding to Him in prayer and worship.

WEEK 6 | DAY 4

SNACK ON THE GO

Open your Bible and read Colossians 4:15–18.

Paul ends his letter to the believers in Colossae with some very personal instructions, but in the final verse of his epistle, he picks up the pen and writes his own signature. The preceding chapters were most likely dictated to a scribe, but this very last verse reveals that Paul didn't want to send the letter off without including his own handwriting at the end, perhaps both as a stamp of approval and as a personal touch.

As you reflect on your own life, who is someone who has encouraged you in your walk of faith? Write down a few names in the space below.

Take a moment to thank God for them, and then pick one person you can write a letter to. Yes, of course, you could call, or text, or email. But in our technology-driven age, letters have become increasingly rare and special. So take an extra minute today to put pen to paper and share with them one thing you learned in this study in Colossians, and thank them for their investment in your life. As you seal the envelope and post it in the mail, continue praying for them, that they will complete the work the Lord gave them to do.

FEAST AT THE TABLE

FOCUS ON GOD

Open your Bible to Psalm 119:130. Write it out as a prayer to the Lord as you begin your study of His Word today.

ENGAGE THE TEXT

Read Colossians 4:15–18 out loud and write it in the space below.

Write down any immediate observations.

Who does Paul list in this passage, and what does he say about each one?

Who is Nympha? What was her involvement in ministry?

According to verse 16, how was Paul's letter to the Colossians to be presented to the church?

What did he instruct them to do with the letter afterward? Why is this significant?

What does Paul communicate to Archippus? Why would it be significant that this personal instruction would have been read in front of the entire congregation?

ASSESS THE MAIN IDEA

Write out the main idea of this passage in a single sentence. Make it precise, concise, and memorable. (Consider the following question: What are the implications of Christ's sufficiency, even as we serve in our place of spiritual giftedness?)

SPARK TRANSFORMATION

The body of Christ is made up of many members, each serving as the Holy Spirit has gifted her or him, and this truth is beautifully displayed in the ending verses of Colossians. What is your spiritual gift? How has God uniquely equipped you so that His Spirit can work in the world through you? (See Romans 12:6–8 for a sample list of spiritual gifts.)

If you don't yet know your spiritual gift, ask a few trusted mature Christians to tell you what they see you excelling in, and then ask God's Spirit to show you ways to serve that are in line with your giftings. If you do know, examine your current activities in light of your gifts, and ask the Holy Spirit to give you wisdom and insight to determine whether you're serving in your sweet spot (that is, where your gifts intersect with ministry needs) or if there's another direction He would like you to pursue.

TURN TO GOD IN WORSHIP

God did not simply set the world in motion and then step out to let history run its course. He continues to be actively involved in the world through His Spirit working in and through believers. What does this say about God?

What does it mean that Christ is the head of the church and we are the body?

Today, worship God for His faithfulness and for the ways He continues to move in the world as His Spirit moves through His people. Specifically, reflect on the ways He has worked in your life through other believers, and thank Him for His continued love and involvement in the world and in your life.

WEEK 6 | DAY 5

SNACK ON THE GO

You know those Facebook videos that go viral? Whether they're cute baby videos or cat videos or military personnel returning home, there's just something about watching them that makes us want to share that experience with someone else.

The first-century church didn't have Facebook. Obviously. But they did have the same desire to share encouraging content with others. So when they'd receive a letter from Paul or Peter or someone else, not only would they read it, but they'd also share it with other churches around them so that they may be encouraged as well.

> After this letter has been read to you, see that it is also read in the church of the Laodiceans and that you in turn read the letter from Laodicea. **COLOSSIANS 4:16**

They didn't want to keep a good thing to themselves, and they didn't want others to miss out on sound spiritual teaching that would build them up in their faith.

As twenty-first-century Christians, we have at our fingertips a technology that's more powerful than anything the Colossian church could have ever imagined; it can be used to spread the gospel farther and faster than any other tool in history. And yet so often, we use Facebook, Instagram, Snapchat, email, and even text messages to spread meaningless drivel.

Take a look at your feed in the last week. What kind of content do you regularly share?

Are the things you share online pointing your friends and family to the brilliance, beauty, and sufficiency of Jesus?

If yes, what is your motivation in doing so? If not, what is holding you back?

What is one way you can use the internet today to share the good news that Jesus is enough in a creative, gentle, and winsome way? Write it down below, and then go do it.

FEAST AT THE TABLE

FOCUS ON GOD

Open your Bible to Psalm 119:135. Write it out as a prayer to the Lord as you begin your study of His Word today.

ENGAGE THE TEXT

Read Colossians. Yep, the whole book. Again. Preferably out loud. As you read, underline each occurrence of "in Christ."

What common themes do you see?

Summarize, in a simple sentence, the meaning of the collective "in Christ" references.

Now list everything that is "with Christ." What common themes do you see?

When does the first "with Christ" show up in the book of Colossians?

Summarize, in a simple sentence, what is true about being "with Christ"?

How many "in Christ" references appear before the first "with Christ"?

What's the significance of Paul taking the time to explain the truths "in Christ" before turning his attention to "with Christ"?

In what way does "in Christ" lay a foundation for the "with Christ" discussion?

Take a moment to review your notes from the past six weeks. How does this conversation about "in Christ"/"with Christ" help you understand the bigger picture of what's going on in these first two chapters of Colossians?

We've zoomed in to the verses and themes of each chapter, and now it's time to zoom out and see how all those ideas work together to form the whole of Paul's letter to the church in Colossae. As you read, consider: Which themes jump off the page at you?

Which verses seem to encapsulate Paul's main ideas?

As you've read Colossians again today, how has your understanding of the book changed compared to when we first started studying this book?

What else stands out to you?

ASSESS THE MAIN IDEA

How would you summarize the book of Colossians? Write out the main idea in a single sentence. Make it precise, concise, and memorable, something that you can easily explain to a friend two years from now.

Consider writing the main idea in your Bible, somewhere you'll be reminded whenever you turn to read a verse in Colossians.

SPARK TRANSFORMATION

What favorite verses from Colossians will you carry with you?

What was a favorite passage from this study?

What new things have you learned about Jesus throughout this study?

What did you learn about yourself?

How does the truth that "Jesus is enough" affect your day-to-day life?

What changes have you seen in your life over the last six weeks through daily "spark transformations"?

TURN TO GOD IN WORSHIP

How have you grown in your knowledge of Jesus these last six weeks? Your love of Jesus? Write a prayer responding to Him in the space below.

WEEKEND REFLECTION—WHERE DO WE GO FROM HERE?

Well, you did it! You finished studying the book of Colossians whether in small snacks at a time or FEASTing on the text or a little bit of both. Reaching the end of a Bible study is both exciting and a bit disorienting. You might be wondering, "Where do I go from here?"

First of all, I encourage you to take a few minutes to reflect on your Bible study experience these last six weeks. How have you grown in your love and knowledge of Jesus?

In what ways has He challenged you to trust that He is enough?

How is He inviting you to live in and through Jesus in this next season of your life?

After studying the book of Colossians, what do you most want to say to God?

You've likely learned a thing or two about how to study the Bible these last six weeks, and you might have even learned what helps you be consistent in your Bible study. I encourage you to download the Quiet Time Evaluation and Plan to help you evaluate what's working and what's not, and plan for consistency in your next season of Quiet Time and Bible study. Simply go to **myOneThingAlone.com/quiet-time-evaluation**.

If your affection for Jesus and His Word has deepened over the last six weeks, that's great news! It means His Holy Spirit is stirring in you a hunger and a desire for Him, and He promises that when we draw near to Him, He will draw near to us (James 4:8). What a wonderful promise!

Secondly, connect with others in your local church and look for ways to serve and continue to grow. I invite you to also join us at myOneThingAlone, an online community of women who love Jesus and grow deeper with Him through creative spiritual disciplines. Like I mentioned in the introduction of this book, myOneThingAlone is where I pioneered the FEAST method of Bible study and where I developed the original version of this study on Colossians, and we're always trying out new and creative ways to grow closer to Jesus together. We would love to have you! Join us at myOneThingAlone.com.

Lastly, I would love for you to share this study with someone who needs it. If this Bible study has helped you grow in your love and knowledge of Jesus, what would it look like to offer that same invitation to another person?

Maybe you could bring together a new group of women in your home or church and lead them through this study you've just completed. Or perhaps you're more of a one-on-one person, and you could reach out to someone to study this book together over coffee each week. Or maybe you invite a few friends around the country to join you in a private Facebook group or via text message to study Colossians together.

Whatever your next steps look like, I pray you will continue to live in and help others discover the fullness of Jesus. Because Jesus is enough not just here and now, but for all eternity to come. What a treat it will be someday to swap stories of how He's met us in our brokenness and filled us up with His fullness. I can't wait to hear them all!

With much joy,

Asheritah

DAILY MAIN IDEAS GUIDE

WEEK ONE, DAY ONE

A survey reading of the book to introduce main themes and key ideas.

WEEK ONE, DAY TWO

Col. 1:1–2: Christ's substitutionary death declares believers holy before God, and His Spirit continually works out that holiness through faith.

WEEK ONE, DAY THREE

Col. 1:3–8: The Holy Spirit transforms people into hope-based, faith-filled, and love-moved believers in Jesus Christ through the gospel.

WEEK ONE, DAY FOUR

Col. 1:9–12: Christ's grace meets people where they are but doesn't leave them as they are; the gospel of Jesus bears fruit in the lives of believers through the power of His Spirit.

WEEK ONE, DAY FIVE

Col. 1:12–14: God the Father rescues unbelievers from the kingdom of darkness into His kingdom of light through Jesus Christ, whose inheritance they now share.

WEEK TWO, DAY ONE

Col. 1:15–20: Jesus Christ is the image of the invisible God and all God's powers and attributes dwell in Him.

WEEK TWO, DAY TWO

Col. 1:21–23: God reconciles unbelievers to Himself through Jesus and regenerates them through a deeper knowledge of and love for Jesus.

WEEK TWO, DAY THREE

Col. 1:24: Paul rejoiced in living out his life mission through deeper knowledge of both the power of Jesus' resurrection and the fellowship of His sufferings.

WEEK TWO, DAY FOUR

Col. 1:24–27: God's mystery is revealed to the saints; namely, that the fullness of Jesus Christ indwells Jews and Gentiles who believe in Him.

WEEK TWO, DAY FIVE

Col. 1:28–2:5: Paul's goal is to bring Christians to full spiritual maturity though a personal knowledge of Jesus Christ.

WEEK THREE, DAY ONE

Col. 2:6–7: Believers live the fullness of Jesus by being rooted and built up in Him, strengthened in faith, and overflowing with thankfulness.

WEEK THREE, DAY TWO

Col. 2:8–10: Believers guard against false teaching by being enamored with Jesus Christ.

WEEK THREE, DAY THREE

Col. 2:11–15: Believers in Jesus partake in His fullness through His circumcision of the heart, forgiveness of their sins, and cancellation of their debts.

WEEK THREE, DAY FOUR

Col. 2:16–23: Jesus' finished work also delivers believers from legalistic requirements, freeing them to live for Him alone. True humility is rooted in our awareness of God's greatness and our neediness, and leads to submission to Jesus and only Jesus.

WEEK THREE, DAY FIVE

Reflection Day: Halfway through our study, readers pause to reflect on what they've learned so far about Jesus and dig deeper into His names and titles, setting the foundation for the second half of the study.

WEEK FOUR, DAY ONE

Col. 3:1–4: Because our eternity is secure in Jesus, we can live out our daily life in the holiness that is already ours in Him.

WEEK FOUR, DAY TWO

Col. 3:5–11: Jesus' return compels us to live out practically what is already true of us positionally, and that is a life conformed to the image of God through knowledge of Jesus.

WEEK FOUR, DAY THREE

Col. 3:12–14: The holiness of God calls His children to lives of holiness inwardly and outwardly.

WEEK FOUR, DAY FOUR

Col. 3:15: Jesus Christ's peace powerfully transforms bitterness and restlessness into unity and thankfulness.

WEEK FOUR, DAY FIVE

Col. 3:16–17: In light of Christ's sufficiency, Christians can and should live outward lives of radical love and inward lives of radical peace.

WEEK FIVE, DAY ONE

Col. 3:18–19: Christ's love moves believers to honor each other in marriage.

WEEK FIVE, DAY TWO

Col. 3:20–21: Christ's love moves believers to honor each other in parent-child relationships.

WEEK FIVE, DAY THREE

Col. 3:22–4:1: Motivated by Christ's real presence and God's already-secured pleasure, Christians can work at the most menial tasks with fullness of joy.

WEEK FIVE, DAY FOUR

Col. 4:2: Jesus' sovereignty moves believers to watchfulness and thankfulness in their prayers.

WEEK FIVE, DAY FIVE

Col. 4:3–4: Devoted to prayer, believers boldly and graciously invite onlookers to join God's family.

WEEK SIX, DAY ONE

Col. 4:5–6: Christ's sufficiency spills into our daily lives through our interactions and conversations with each other.

WEEK SIX, DAY TWO

Col. 4:7–9: Jesus' lordship frees Christians to serve one another without fear.

WEEK SIX, DAY THREE

Col. 4:10–14: Empowered by the Spirit and under the headship of Jesus Christ, Christians serve each other in the body of Christ.

WEEK SIX, DAY FOUR

Col. 4:15–18: Having received God's generous grace in Jesus, believers serve generously and graciously, reaching out and bringing in, fulfilling their mission.

WEEK SIX, DAY FIVE

Colossians summary: At the conclusion of our study, participants read the entire book of Colossians once again to see how all the themes come together to comprise the unifying message of the book, which is: because Jesus Christ is the fullness of God, believers are united with Him in spiritual, relational, and missional fullness.

SERVING AND LEADING:
Devotional Guide for Leaders

Dear women's leader,

Being in a position of leadership comes with soul-soaring rewards and stay-up-all-night responsibilities, dreams, and worries unique to this servant role. Whether you're leading one precious woman across a coffee shop table or a thousand women in an auditorium, I've written the following pages with you in mind, dear one.

These devotional prompts are meant to take you deeper in your own personal study of the Word after you've completed the FEAST sections each day. But as I've said before, if you skip a day or two (or ten), there is grace for the weary. Come back and pick up with the current day's prompts. Together we'll tackle some of the sticky and sensitive parts of leadership, always redirecting our hearts to Jesus—the ultimate Servant Leader—for He is enough both in our ministries and in our own lives.

If you can, I encourage you to find another woman in leadership to go through this study together, as you may find yourself wanting to discuss your answers with someone else who understands. And if you're feeling lonely in this calling, allow me to reissue my invitation earlier in this book to you in particular: myOneThingAlone.com is a community that welcomes women in all seasons of life, and that includes you too.

My prayer for you today and throughout the following weeks is that you would find refreshment for your own soul and encouragement in your ministry that you might labor with all the energy Christ so powerfully works in you. For His kingdom, and His renown.

With much joy,

Asheritah

WEEK ONE, DAY ONE

Read John 13:1–5. How does Jesus demonstrate servant leadership?

How does Paul demonstrate this same characteristic in his letter to the Colossians?

What does servant leadership look like in your own life?

As you begin this study, write out a prayer asking the Lord to reveal ways that you can grow in servanthood in your own leadership.

WEEK ONE, DAY TWO

What a blessing it is to have access to Paul's pastoral letters to first-century churches! While much of what's written addresses specific challenges they were facing there and then, the central truths apply to our lives here and now as well.

Have you ever considered writing letters to the women you serve? They don't need to be theological treatises, but a simple note in which you remind them of God's eternal truths. You could even take what you learn each day in your study of Colossians and write a sentence or two to encourage them. You might be surprised how powerful this expression of love and care can be.

Over the next few weeks, prayerfully consider writing your own brief epistles, even if they take the form of emails or texts. Just as He encouraged and strengthened those in the early church, God is pleased to use our words today to encourage those He has entrusted in our care.

WEEK ONE, DAY THREE

As women in ministry, we often get to see the behind-the-scenes of church life. And while much of it may be exhilarating, we can also see and experience some very hurtful things. After a while, it's easy to get discouraged and become critical. We've all seen ministers of the Word who are burned out and sadly burn out others as well.

Paul was familiar with disappointment in ministry. We get a glimpse of his hurt in Colossians 4:10–11, when he sends greetings from Aristarchus, Mark, and Justus, who are, he notes, "the only Jews among my co-workers for the kingdom of God." There's a tinge of sadness in those words, even if these same men have proved a comfort to him.

And even the circumstances that prompted Paul to write this letter were discouraging. The Colossians were falling for all kinds of heretical teachings instead of holding on to the truth of the gospel of Jesus. There's much that would cause his heart to sink.

Yet notice that Paul fixes his attention on all the good he sees in the Colossians: their faith, their love for others, the fruit of the gospel. Paul chooses a heart of gratitude and thanksgiving (1:3) even as he prays that God would mature them (1:9) He dwells on those things that are lovely, admirable, excellent, and praiseworthy (see Phil. 4:8) instead of allowing negativity and discouragement to weigh him down.

In your own ministry and church life, make it a habit of praising God for all the good things He's doing in the lives of the women you serve or who are in your Bible study with you. Brainstorm a list of those things in the space below.

Absolutely, there are opportunities to pray that they may continue to grow and mature, but don't forget to celebrate what He's already accomplished and what He's continuing to do. This type of gratitude in ministry will guard your heart from bitterness and fill your prayers with sweet blessings.

WEEK ONE, DAY FOUR

One of the most powerful ways to serve people in our lives is to pray God's Word over them, boldly proclaiming spiritual blessings over them.

Identify two to five people you directly influence and commit to praying for them over the next six weeks.

Then consider writing down Scripture-saturated prayers inspired by Colossians 1:9–12, as well as other Pauline prayers like Ephesians 3:16–19, Philippians 1:9–11, or Ephesians 1:17–19a. You can write them in the space below, or you may want to write them on notecards you can carry with you. Not only will those people you pray for be blessed, but you will find yourself growing in your confidence and Scripture vocabulary in prayer as well.

WEEK ONE, DAY FIVE

Unfortunately, Christians are often shaped more by secular outlets and contorted ideas about Christianity instead of being transformed by the timeless truths of the Bible. This is certainly no new development.

Paul had his finger on the pulse of contemporary culture and was able to speak knowledgeably about the issues these early churches were facing.

Do you know what media outlets are shaping the women of your church? What blogs are they reading? Who are they watching on live video? What podcasts are they listening to? We'd like to think that everyone who teaches from a "Christian" platform teaches sound doctrine, but sadly that's not the case.

Take some time today to discover the voices shaping this generation's minds and hearts, and ask God's Spirit to give you wisdom and humility as you sift through the teachings. And if you find something that does not line up with Scripture, be brave to refute these wrong declarations and point your students to the timeless truth of God's Word.

WEEK TWO, DAY ONE

One of the temptations of the modern-day church is to segregate worship and study, as if they were two separate disciplines instead of two sides of the same coin. We do our women a disservice if we lead them to accumulate head knowledge that doesn't transform their hearts and affections. Sure, knowledge of God and Scripture is important. We live in an age of biblical illiteracy, and we do well to guide women to study the Bible. After all, that's what we're doing through this book.

But if our study of Scripture ends in accumulation of Bible trivia, we've missed the point. God created us to worship Him, and the purpose of Bible study ought always to be worship. This is why we conclude each FEAST session with a call to turn to God in worship.

As you reflect on the ways you lead other women in the study of God's Word, how might you encourage them to grow in their adoration and personal worship of Jesus?

How could you guide your students of Scripture to see and recognize Jesus in every chapter of Scripture? How could you help them see Jesus in the pages of their Bibles, not only when the text is clearly about Him, as it is in today's passage, but also when His presence is more implicit?

If this is a struggle for you personally, a wonderful resource is *The Jesus Storybook Bible* by Sally Lloyd-Jones, as it helps readers learn how "every story whispers His name," or on a more academic level, *Jesus in the Bible* by Kenneth Boa.

This discipline of combining study and worship is as true about the New Testament as it is about the Old Testament. This was what Jesus told the disciples on the road to Emmaus in Luke 24:13–36. Consider this quote from Dr. Iain Duguid, professor of Old Testament at Westminster Theological Seminary:

> The Old Testament is not primarily a book about ancient history or culture, though it contains many things that are historical and that describe ancient cultures. Centrally, the Old Testament is a book about Christ, and more specifically, about his sufferings and the glories that will follow—that is, it is a book about the promise of a coming Messiah through whose sufferings God will establish his glorious, eternal kingdom.[17]

WEEK TWO, DAY TWO

It is unusual for Paul to name himself in the middle of one of his letters, but here in verse 23, he calls himself a "servant" of the gospel of Christ. This word for servant is familiar to many of us as the Greek word *diákonos*, from which we draw our modern word *deacon* and is also sometimes translated minister. It "properly means 'to kick up dust' as one *running an errand*" for one's master.[18]

That one moment when Paul met Jesus on the Damascus Road (Acts 9:1–19) radically transformed him for life, and he dedicated his life to spreading the good news about Jesus to the Gentile world. That was his lifelong errand, and he literally kicked up dust as he went from one place to another in service to the gospel.

In your own life as a minister, do you feel your duties and projects clearly flow from and advance the gospel?

Today, take some time to pray over your agenda, and rededicate yourself as a servant to do your Master's bidding.

WEEK TWO, DAY THREE

This passage, and the related cross-references, give us a glimpse of the suffering Paul endured on behalf of the first-century church. His was not an easy ministry, nor was it marked with affirmation and accolades. On the contrary, he suffered much opposition in proclaiming the gospel. But take a look at 1 Corinthians 2:4–5 and 1 Thessalonians 1:5–6.

In Paul's example, we see that true ministry is a life poured out for those we serve, not just a message preached for those who come to listen. Ministry is labor. It's misunderstanding. It's opening our own lives for people to see the power of God in our weaknesses, our suffering, our lack, our "misfitness."

Sure, we may teach God's Word, and there's power in His Word going out. But more than listening to our words, our people will watch our lives. And sometimes it's the mundane ministry that matters the most—not the big events, not the flashy names, not the impressive credentials, but the Tuesday afternoon faithfulness, the gentle response, the steadfastness in the midst of being misunderstood. Don't discredit the small things. Those are often what the Holy Spirit uses in the biggest ways.

WEEK TWO, DAY FOUR

False teachers peddling a "secret knowledge" about God are nothing new. They baited the first-century church and they continue to bait people today, though their propositions may sound slightly different. In every age of the church, there's a danger of being led astray by "fine-sounding arguments" (2:4), and that's just as true today.

From extrabiblical "revelations" written in comforting devotional form to gematria—a mysterious way of interpreting Scripture that assigns numerical values to words, names, or phrases of the Bible in the belief that words or phrases with identical numerical values bear relation to each other and reveal mysteries of God—Christians today face many temptations to take their eyes off Christ and become distracted by "hollow and deceptive philosophy, which depends on human tradition and the elemental spiritual forces of this world rather than on Christ" (2:8). *And the danger lies in getting wrapped up in things about God instead of being enamored with God, as revealed in Christ Jesus.*

Ask God to help you recognize the philosophies that are assaulting the women you serve, and to give you wisdom to refute them with His Word, always pointing them back to Jesus. This may seem like a daunting task, but remember that "Christ in you, the hope of glory" assures you of access to all His heavenly riches, and all wisdom and understanding found in Him. Write below a prayer asking for His help to keep pointing women to Jesus, as He is revealed in Scripture.

WEEK TWO, DAY FIVE

One of the common temptations for those of us in ministry is to find our worth and our identity in what we do for God. And truly, there is a call on our lives to bear fruit in good works. Absolutely.

But today's passage reminds us that God is the One who works in and through us. We are conduits of His power and grace when we make ourselves available to Him. So there's a beautiful tension of "strenuously contend[ing]" in ministry, but doing it from a place of spiritual rest, knowing that it's actually Christ's energy that works powerfully.

As we head into the weekend, consider what your labor looks like. Are you drawing on your own energy or on Christ's? Go back through the last chapter and notice the relationship between Paul's laboring and Christ's accomplishing. Who does the actual work of ministry? What would it look like to do the work of ministry from a place of rest, confident that God will handle the results?

WEEK THREE, DAY ONE

So often writers in the Bible use the imagery of a tree or plant to illustrate the believer's life and fruitfulness (see Pss. 1:3; 52:8; 92:12–14; Isa. 44:3–4; 61:3; Jer. 17:7–8; Matt. 13:8, 23; 21:33–34, 43). And just as plants go through different stages of growth, so we know that believers also grow in their faith, starting as sprouting seeds, developing into young saplings, putting down deep roots as young trees, and developing towering branches, bearing abundant fruit, and reproducing as their seed is carried to new soils.

So also, the women we minister to are in different seasons of their spiritual lives. Some have yet to receive Jesus as Lord. Others have received Him but have shallow roots and need to go deeper. Others still are going through a growth spurt. Some may need strengthening, and others might be overflowing with fruit. While all these characteristics are true of each of us—to varying degrees at every stage of our spiritual journey—sometimes the women we serve need help understanding their stage in life and how to grow best in their current season.

I've developed a free tool to help you and the women in your church assess where they are in their spiritual journey and what steps to take next. Go to **myOneThingAlone.com/spiritual-assessment** to find a Spiritual Growth Assessment and help women grow right where they are.

WEEK THREE, DAY TWO

Women today are bombarded with messages that are diametrically opposed and yet both wrong: either they're told all the ways that they are not enough or their self-esteem is built up in a false empowerment. Yet Paul speaks to both these errors, reminding us that our value and identity come not from ourselves or our accomplishments but from Christ.

As you encounter women in your ministry who suffer from low self-esteem, how can you point them to the fullness that is theirs in Jesus? And for those who may have an inflated sense of self, how can you point them to the fullness that is found only in Jesus?

WEEK THREE, DAY THREE

As mentioned in the study, so many of us carry an unwritten list in our hearts of all the ways we've failed. We might know in our minds that Jesus nailed our list to the cross, but we keep climbing up there, tearing it down, rolling it up, and carrying it around as if it's still ours. It's hard to believe we're really forgiven.

How might you help the women you serve bring their list to the cross and leave it there?

Sometimes physically acting out spiritual truths can help us visualize what's real, and step into that reality instead of holding to the past. If you're studying this passage with a small group in your church, consider this exercise: have women write down the sins of their past they can't let go of, and spend some time in private confession and prayer. Then invite them to fold up their list and nail (or thumb tack) it to a cross you've set up to the side of the room. Invite them to kneel at the cross and visualize Jesus doing this very thing with their list, and encourage them to release their past and receive the forgiveness and freedom that is theirs in Christ. Afterward, discreetly dispose of the lists, shredding or burning them to ensure their past remains in the past.

WEEK THREE, DAY FOUR

Learn about the Jewish festivals. How did they point to Jesus? Which ones were already fulfilled in Jesus? How might you use these festivities to lead the women around you into a deeper understanding of Jesus the Messiah? Consider inviting one or two friends to join you in celebrating a Jewish festival, not to impress God or to gain righteousness, but to deepen your understanding of Jesus the Messiah, and how He fulfilled all the requirements of the Law. For ideas, visit JewsforJesus.org.[19]

WEEK THREE, DAY FIVE

We're halfway through our study. How are your women doing?

How are you doing? Are you consistently feeding your soul from God's Word? If not, what's standing in the way?

What changes do you need to make to be more consistent in your intake of Scripture for your own spiritual growth? How can you develop rhythms of worship and rest to feed yourself before you try to feed others? Journal your thoughts below.

WEEK FOUR, DAY ONE

A common temptation in ministry is to equate our value with our accomplishments. How many women attended the special event this past spring? How many new faces showed up to Bible study last week? How much money did you raise as a group for foreign missions? Sometimes the stakes can seem so high, and we almost crumble under the pressure.

And while all those things may be good, they can become dangerous when we tie our sense of identity and worth to what we've done. You are not what you do. You are not the sum of your achievements. Nor are you defined by your failures.

You are Christ's. You have been raised with Christ, your life is hidden with Christ, you are seated with Christ (Eph. 2:6), and you will also appear with Christ in glory when He appears. Allow these truths to become the safety net beneath your feet as you walk the high beam of public ministry. No matter what the results of your work, you are His, and He is enough.

Set your mind and heart on Him.

WEEK FOUR, DAY TWO

Whether others put us there or we've climbed our way to the top, many of us find ourselves on a pedestal, perching precariously as others alternately look up to us and peer critically at us. No one likes to admit their failures, least of all those of us in ministry, especially when we're already under close scrutiny.

But is it possible that we're being dishonest by plastering on a smile and hiding our failures and insecurities? "Do not lie to each other," Paul exhorts his listeners in today's passage. How many of us, when asked how we're doing, answer with a nonchalant, "Oh, fine. Thank you. How are you?" Even though we screamed in anger at the kids on the way to church, spoke unkindly of someone to our husband, and harbor bitterness toward that other ministry leader who was chosen as guest speaker in our place.

Friends, let us quit the pretense. We are not fine. We are broken women in need of a Savior. We are women just like those we serve, who have taken off our old self but are still learning what it means to put on the new self. We don't have it all together. So let's stop pretending we do.

Instead, let us dare to be transparent as appropriate, sharing how our own struggles and insecurities bring us to our knees before Jesus. Admitting our failures and and receiving His grace. Being brave enough to acknowledge, "I'm not perfect, but I know Someone who is, and I'd love for us to walk together as we become renewed into the image of Jesus."

Christ is enough, so we can be honest with each other as we live out our transformations.

WEEK FOUR, DAY THREE

You are chosen. You are holy. You are dearly loved.

Allow those words to sink into your heart for a moment.

Chosen. Holy. Loved.

This is who you are, my friend, and this is the reality that God is calling you to step into. It's already true about you positionally. Now God is inviting you to step into your identity practically.

Just as God called the Israelites to be His chosen people, holy among the heathen nations, so He has called us, Jesus' bride, to be His own special people.

What would it look like for you to do ministry if you fully believed and lived out this identity in Christ? How would you work differently? Fail differently? Love differently?

You are chosen, holy, and loved, because Christ is all, and is in all. Worship Him today.

WEEK FOUR, DAY FOUR

Women, we're good at worrying.

We'll worry about everything from what others think of us to what our loved ones are doing and everything in between.

And as women in ministry, we not only shoulder our own share of worries, but we're often burdened with others' worries too. Of course, we're called to carry one another's burdens. That's part of being one body.

But perhaps we, or the women we serve, struggle with needless worry. And, let's be honest, Scripture is pretty clear that worry is a sin—it indicates a heart that is restless, that does not trust. It's interesting to note in our passage that Paul follows up his exhortation to being ruled by Jesus' peace with a brief but firm instruction to be thankful.

How might thankfulness be the antidote to worry in your life?

What might it look like for you to speak peace over needless worry, both in your own life and in the lives of the women you serve?

WEEK FOUR, DAY FIVE

Today's passage is an important reminder that whatever we teach needs to be grounded in the truth of Scripture and pointing to Jesus Christ.

But it's also a reminder that, as teachers, we need to be digging into God's Word for ourselves, feasting at the table before we can feed others around us. After all, you won't get far on an empty stomach, and words spoken from a parched and dry soul simply will not resonate as those spoken from the abundance of feasting on the Bread of Life.

But even more than the impact this has on *others* we serve, allowing Christ's message to dwell among us richly affects *us* at the deepest heart level. What is His message? Write it in the space below.

Ask the Holy Spirit, are you allowing Christ's message to dwell in you richly?

WEEK FIVE, DAY ONE

Few passages cause as much grief to married women as Colossians 3:18–19 and its parallel passages. Why do you think this is?

How does a proper understanding of the word "submit" transform the way wives ought to relate to their husbands?

As you've studied this passage, are there any faces that come to mind? Women in your ministry who are in a difficult season in their marriage? Write their names in the space below or in a prayer journal as a reminder to pray for them.

How might you encourage them today?

WEEK FIVE, DAY TWO

There's something exhilarating about being in ministry: being wanted and needed, feeling important enough that someone would call on you and want your input. And in contrast, the daily tasks of a family—like driving kids to soccer practice or packing lunches—seem, well, kind of inconsequential. There's a certain feeling of importance that comes from doing ministry, and a certain feeling of invisibility from doing the mundane tasks of life. And sadly, it's easy to get sucked into the vortex of endless ministry duties, sacrificing our families on the altar of ministry. I'll be honest: this is a constant struggle for me too.

These passages in Colossians 3:18–21 remind us that each of us has an important role in the lives of our family, and no one else can fill that role. Others can file paperwork, send emails, and have coffee chats. Others can teach Bible study and counsel women. But if you're a wife and/or mom, only you can fill those spaces in your loved ones' lives. And that's a privilege we can easily take for granted.

As you consider these instructions to husbands, wives, parents, and children, what does this look like in your own life?

Spend some time in quiet contemplation and prayer, and ask the Lord to reveal to you how you can prioritize the crucial roles He's given you in this private ministry of serving your family, while still honoring the public ministry He's given you as well.

WEEK FIVE, DAY THREE

While the vast majority of women in our church will have never experienced slavery, most of us have probably worked for supervisors who have shown favoritism or unfairness at one point or another.

How does this passage inspire perseverance in doing good, even when those who supervise us do not notice or care?

Write a prayer, asking God to help you work for His approval alone and to help you encourage others to do the same. Surrender your expectations to Him in the space below.

WEEK FIVE, DAY FOUR

"Devote yourselves to prayer," Paul instructs.

Take an honest assessment of your prayer life. How often do you pray for yourself, your family, your ministry, your surroundings?

Ask the Holy Spirit how might you grow in your devotion to prayer.

These questions are not meant to heap guilt or condemnation on you, or give you yet another thing to do to fill up your busy schedule. But rather, let's ask the Lord to reveal to us how we might better lean into His energy, His strength, His insight for the daily duties set before us. Write a prayer in the space below.

Consider also how you might challenge the women in your church to devote themselves to regular prayer. Could you invite them to an hour-long prayer meeting in your home? Write your ideas below.

WEEK FIVE, DAY FIVE

This passage is a brief insight into how Paul prayed for his ministry. In the space below, write out your own prayer based on Colossians 4:3–4.

WEEK SIX, DAY ONE

Gossip. It's present in too many women's church meetings I've attended. And although I know gossip is a sin and try to stay away from it, I feel tongue-tied when it comes to addressing it when others gossip in a conversation I'm a part of. And sadly, it's the way we talk to and about each other that often turns unbelievers away in disgust.

It can be so subtle, coming up in the guise of prayer requests and other innocent chitchat in church hallways, but it's deadly. As we look at today's passage, what instruction does Paul offer for our conversations?

How can we make sure our own speech is full of grace and seasoned with salt when addressing gossip and other verbal sins?

WEEK SIX, DAY TWO

In this passage, we see a fascinating leadership intervention, as Paul uses his relational clout to reconcile two dear brothers in Christ. Take a closer look at the letter to Philemon. In what ways does Paul put himself on the line?

How does he frame his appeal to Philemon? What is his tone in this letter? How does Paul figuratively don the towel of humility to serve both Onesimus and Philemon?

In your own leadership role, how can you use your position to bend down and serve those in relational conflict?

How might your humility nudge others toward humble and loving responses? Ask the Lord to keep your heart sensitive to ways you may serve those you lead in relational reconciliation.

WEEK SIX, DAY THREE

As we look at Paul's list of fellow workers for the gospel, it's interesting to see Luke listed there. Luke was well-educated in Greek culture, a doctor by profession, probably a Gentile by birth. He's also the writer of the gospel of Luke and the Acts of the Apostles. His writing reveals outstanding command of the Greek language, and his vocabulary indicates impressive geographical and cultural familiarity.

Paul would have had every reason to be jealous of Luke, or to compare his ministry to Luke's. After all, it's not uncommon for those of us who serve in ministry in one way or another to suffer from *comparisonitis*. If you think of it, Luke wrote a gospel and Paul didn't. Luke knew people that Paul didn't. Luke had a classical education that Paul didn't.

But instead of allowing insecurities to distance them, Paul invited Luke to come alongside him and minister together. He recognized that they each had individual strengths and could be used uniquely by God in ministry. And so we see that Luke becomes Paul's companion on his missionary journeys and in his two-year imprisonment in Rome (see Acts 28). Take a closer look at Colossians 4:14. How does Paul describe Luke? What does this term reveal about his disposition toward Luke?

As you look at your own life, who are you tempted to compare yourself to? How does this affect your heart and your ministry?

What would it look like for you to reach out and link arms with these women and men instead of allowing jealousy or competition to cripple you?

In the space below, write a prayer asking the Lord to help you unite with other coworkers in ministry and do His work together.

WEEK SIX, DAY FOUR

At the end of Paul's instructions to all the believers in Colossae, he adds a very personal note to a man named Archippus. In the space below, write out Colossians 4:17.

We don't know much about Archippus or why Paul would remind him to complete his work, but turn to Philemon verse 2 and make a note of what words Paul uses to describe him. What would this term reveal about his involvement in ministry?

Turn to 2 Timothy 4:5 and write it in the space below.

How are the instructions similar? How are they different?

As you reflect on your own life, what might the Lord's instruction to you look like today? Write it in the space below, then respond to Him with a prayer of your own.

WEEK SIX, DAY FIVE

The end of an in-depth study is both exhilarating and a bit disorienting. Some women may find themselves asking, "Where do I go next?" Perhaps you've asked yourself that same question when you've come to the end of a structured study.

Today, take ten minutes to reflect on your Bible study experience these last six weeks, specifically your quiet time plan, or the way you regularly spend time with and in the Word. Ask the Holy Spirit to give you insight and wisdom as you answer the following questions:

What's working well with your quiet time plan?

What challenges did you face over the last six weeks, and how did they affect your time spent in the Word?

What challenges do you anticipate coming up in this next season?

What do you need to adjust, or what's something new you can try?

What is your plan for including worship and prayer in your quiet time with God?

As you reflect on your observations above, how do you plan to spend time with Jesus each day?

After studying the book of Colossians, what do you want to say to God?

As you lead your women at the end of this study, encourage them to spend some time doing this same exercise, evaluating what has gone well and what challenges they've faced in their Bible study over the past six weeks. Celebrate achievements and brainstorm creative solutions to common challenges. Encourage those you lead to develop a simple plan to continue growing in God's Word, whether snacking or FEASTing, and remind them of the supremacy and sufficiency of Jesus: He is enough.

NOTES

1 Douglas J. Moo, *The Letters to the Colossians and to Philemon*, The Pillar New Testament Commentary (Grand Rapids: Eerdmans, 2008), 27.

2. Peter J. Gorday, ed., Thomas C. Oden, gen. ed., *Colossians, 1–2 Thessalonians, 1–2 Timothy, Titus, Philemon: Ancient Christian Commentary on Scripture* (Downers Grove, IL: InterVarsity Press, 2000), 6.

3. Roy B. Zuck and John F. Walvoord, *The Bible Knowledge Commentary: New Testament* (Colorado Springs: David C. Cook, 1983), 670–71.

4. Note for Colossians 1:14, *NIV Study Bible* (Grand Rapids, Zondervan, 1995).

5. John MacArthur, *The MacArthur Bible Commentary* (Nashville: Thomas Nelson, 2005), 1733.

6. Basil the Great, *Homilies on the Hexameron* 9.6, in Gorday and Oden, *Ancient Christian Commentary on Scripture*, 11.

7. Novatian, *On the Trinity* 18.1–3, in ibid., 12.

8. Michael Martin, "Letter to the Colossians," in *Holman Illustrated Bible Dictionary*, Chad Brand, Charles Draper, and Archie England, gen. eds. (Nashville: B&H Publishing, 2015), 319.

9. Zuck and Walvoord, *The Bible Knowledge Commentary*, 675.

10. Note for Colossians 2:8, *NIV Study Bible*.

11. R. Dennis Cole, "Circumcision," in *Holman Illustrated Bible Dictionary*, 296.

12. Moo, *The Letters to the Colossians and Philemon*, 227.

13. Asheritah Ciuciu, *Unwrapping the Names of Jesus: An Advent Devotional* (Chicago: Moody, 2017), 56.

14. Moo, *The Letters to the Colossians and to Philemon*, 306.

15. Ibid., 308.

16. Ralph Gower explains, "Meals were an important aspect of friendship. To eat a meal with someone was to be at peace with him (Genesis 26:28–30). Salt had a particular function as part of the meal. To 'eat salt' was to be at peace—perhaps because it healed wounds (Mark 9:50; when Jesus tells us to be 'salty,' he is therefore telling us to be at peace with others)" (Ralph Gower, *The New Manners and Customs of Bible Times* [Chicago: Moody, 2005], 218).

17. Iain Duguid, "Four Principles for Reading the Old Testament," https://faculty.wts.edu/posts/seeingchrist/.

18. A. T. Robertson, quoted in HELPS Word-studies, on "1249. diakonos," Bible Hub; Thayer's Greek Lexicon; http://biblehub.com/greek/1249.htm.

19. These books will also enhance your understanding of Jesus the Christ by showing how the richness and symbolism of Old Testament celebrations including the Sabbath point to Him: *Christ in the Passover* by Ceil and Moishe Rosen; *Christ in the Feast of Tabernacles* by David Brickner; *Christ in the Feast of Pentecost* by David Brickner and Rich Robinson; *Christ in the Sabbath* by Rich Robinson.

ACKNOWLEDGMENTS

To the founding members of myOneThingAlone.com: you helped pioneer this snack/FEAST approach to Bible study, and you supported me with your enthusiasm for our first original Colossians study, your suggestions for improvements, and your testimonies of how God used it in your life. Without you, this book would never have reached the printing press. Thank you for journeying with me as we invite women around the world to find joy in Jesus. You are my people.

To Tawny: you perfectly balance the roles of agent, friend, and confidant. Thank you for knowing when to urge me forward and when to graciously pull me back. You're a special blessing.

To Judy, Connor, Ashley, Erik, Pam, and the entire Moody Publishers team: you took a rough draft and turned it into a beautiful reality. What a gift it's been to partner together to equip and inspire women to dive deeper into God's Word.

To Flaviu, Kate, Shirley, Emily Ann, and the whole One Thing Alone team: your behind-the-scenes work for our ministry allows me to devote myself to writing and teaching. I couldn't do what I do without you faithfully doing what you do. Thank you from the bottom of my heart.

To Carmen and the Serve Team women of The Chapel in Green: you ladies inspire me each week to serve and lead like Jesus, and you've graciously given me a place to do just that alongside you. I wrote the Devotional Guide for Leaders with you in mind, and I pray it blesses you as you bless the dear women sitting at your tables.

To my Christian Authors Mastermind Group: you are my Tychiuses, my Justuses, and my Epaphrases. Your faithfulness in ministering the Word of God in print and online heartens me, your prayers bolster me, and your humor refreshes me. What a delight to keep serving together for all eternity!

To my darling husband and little ones: you are God's choicest gift in my life. Thank you for grace, laughter, and forgiveness, not only as I've stolen away to finish this study but also as I've bumbled my way through living it out. At home. With you. Where it matters most. You are my greatest treasures and my biggest ministry. I love you.

To my Lord and Love, Jesus: You astound me. My feet had almost slipped when I took my eyes off You. But You are good, and You are faithful, and You keep calling me back to Yourself. Thank You. In Your presence, You fill me to overflowing, and I discover that You're all I really want or need. For You are enough.

MY ONE THING ALONE

MISSED YOUR QUIET TIME?

WISH YOU COULD GO DEEPER IN YOUR BIBLE STUDY?

LONGING FOR ACCOUNTABILITY?

Join a thriving community of women who love Jesus and grow deeper with Him through creative spiritual disciplines.

Through weekly videos and resources delivered right to your inbox, you'll learn to become more

- ☑ consistent in your daily devotions

- ☑ confident in your Bible study skills

- ☑ creative in your personal worship

Go to myOneThingAlone.com/quickstart to learn more and download your free Bible Study Quickstart Guide.

Can the Bible help me with my food struggles?

978-0-8024-1537-0

Whether the struggle is with excess weight, unwanted cravings, total control, or extreme diets, we all have a relationship with food. *Full* unpacks a theology of food to break its power, help us engage food holistically, and free us to taste and see that God is good.

Also available as an eBook

MOODY
Publishers®

From the Word to Life®

How to focus on Christ during Advent

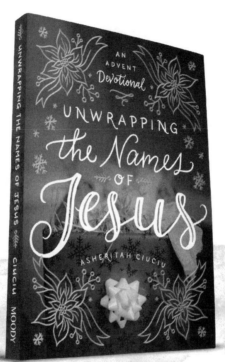

978-0-8024-1672-8

Unwrapping the Names of Jesus leads readers through the four weeks of Advent (Hope, Preparation, Joy, and Love) by focusing each day's reflection on one name of Jesus. Each week begins with an interactive family devotional followed by five daily reflections, as well as suggestions for fun-filled family activities or service projects to enhance a family's Advent experience.

Also available as an eBook

MOODY Publishers®

From the Word to Life®

Bible Studies for Women

IN-DEPTH. CHRIST-CENTERED. REAL IMPACT.

AN UNEXPLAINABLE LIFE
978-0-8024-1473-1

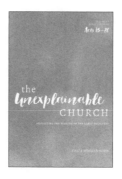

THE UNEXPLAINABLE CHURCH
978-0-8024-1742-8

HIS LAST WORDS
978-0-8024-1467-0

I AM FOUND
978-0-8024-1468-7

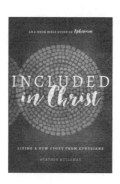

INCLUDED IN CHRIST
978-0-8024-1591-2

THIS I KNOW
978-0-8024-1596-7

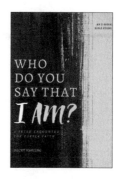

WHO DO YOU SAY THAT I AM?
978-0-8024-1550-9

MOODY Publishers®
From the Word to Life®

Explore our Bible studies
at **moodypublisherswomen.com**

Also available as eBooks